Vol. II

How to Attain Your Desires
How to Live Life and Love It!

By GENEVIEVE BEHREND
With Dr. Joe Vitale

T0154183

JOE VITALE

For information about permission to reproduce
selections from the book, write to Permissions,
Morgan James Publishing, 1225 Franklin Ave Ste 325,
Garden City, NY 11530-1693

ISBN: 1-933596-32-5

MORGAN · JAMES
PUBLISHING FOR THE REST OF US...
www.morganjamespublishing.com

New York

MrFire.com

Vol. II

How to Attain Your Desires
How to Live Life and Love It!

2005

GENEVIEVE BEHREND
JOE VITALE

JOE VITALE

CONTENTS

INTRODUCTION
The Second Lost Treasure

You can't imagine my thrill when I discovered yet another long lost gem by one of my favorite authors. I have always felt that her other rare book, *Attaining Your Desires*, was the Holy Grail of spiritual books. Little did I know that Genevieve Behrend had followed that masterpiece with a second rare volume, the one you are now holding in your hands.

If you know of Genevieve's name, it's most likely because of her famous book, *Your Invisible Power*, which is easily available online and in many book stores. But few people know that she wrote the book I discovered a few years ago and then reprinted, titled *Attaining Your Desires*.

But what even *I* didn't know is that she had also written a continuation of that book. I stumbled across an original first edition of it, read it, loved it, and began to practice what it teaches. I was amazed to see that this second lost treasure was as good if not better than the first one that I published.

I got so excited that I immediately contacted David Hancock of Morgan James Publishing and told him to "Get ready to publish another Genevieve book!"

He stopped everything he was doing, got the printer, the designer and everyone else on board, and the result is this book that you are reading.

Please read this gem and then get copies for others. You and I and everyone else needs to hear this message. While many teachers remind us that we have the power to change our lives, few of them explain it so clearly as this book reveals.

Brace yourself. You're about to create miracles.

Please use your power for good.

Dr. Joe Vitale

Author, *The Attractor Factor*
and way too many other books to list here
See www.MrFire.com

Attaining Your Desires

How to Live Life and Love It!

By

GENEVIEVE BEHREND
only personal pupil of Judge T. Troward

Author of
Your Invisible Power
The Healing Power Is Life
Attaining Your Desires

DEDICATION

To Grace N. Northcutt of Denver, Colorado, whose gracious co-operation enabled the new edition of this book to be printed, this volume is lovingly dedicated by her devoted friend,

Genevieve Behrend

To all those who seek to create heaven on earth.

Dr. Joe Vitale

FOREWORD

The purpose of this series of personal-pointer Lessons, which are herein compiled into one volume, is to indicate in a clear, concise way "the **natural** principles governing the relation between the creative action of all **thought-power** and material **things,**" i.e., circumstances and conditions.

If these few simple principles are carefully studied, and mastered to your satisfaction, and then put into **practical, hourly application**, the student will find very soon that it is possible for man to make **conscious** contact with the Almighty, Ever-Present, Never-Failing God; and this just naturally means individual FREEDOM, freedom from every form of limitation and bondage of any nature. (Read Mark 9:23.) Then try to believe that the Spirit of Life, which is **your** life also, knows "How to Live Life and Love It."

All the joy Life has to give is yours right now! Let us start on the highway to unqualified success now. God is our guide.

Your loving companion,

Genevieve Behrend

LESSON I: LIVE LIFE AND LOVE IT!

MASTER: Let us begin this morning's lesson with the certain knowledge that every living thing really wishes to **enjoy** Life. Once one really has entered into the true Spirit of Life that one can not help loving to live and is certain to enjoy life.

PUPIL: That is just it. If one could get into the Spirit of Living Life, I am sure one, every one, would enjoy it. But it seems to me that the general run of humanity live in the spirit of death rather than of life. The average person I know is always **wishing** that he could but at the same time **knowing that** he **can't**. That does not seem like really living.

MASTER: Indeed that is not living and people who live in that form of mental action are "the living dead." Let us see if we can not find an easy, logical method of entering into the true Spirit of Life. We know that we must enter into the Spirit of a book, or a picture, or of music, else they are entirely meaningless to us. To really appreciate anything we must share the mental attitude of the creative thought and feeling which brought them into outward form.

PUPIL: Now I am wondering if getting into the spirit of a thing would be getting into the spiritual prototype of the thing we may wish to enjoy. For example, I should very much enjoy a home of my own, a husband and children. Can one really get into the spirit of these good things before one does have them, or before one can see them in form?

MASTER: I am pleased that you mention the spiritual prototype is the spiritual, or mental, purpose of a thing, and is the **true place of origin** of anything. So you wish a home, husband, children?

PUPIL: Yes, a home in the country, not a large house, one just large enough that we can live in every room of it.

MASTER: The house is to be the home?

PUPIL: Why yes, of course.

MASTER: I asked this, you see, because just a house may not always be a home while a mere tent may be. Your prototype for the home would be PROTECTION, SHELTER, FREEDOM. To begin at the beginning let us get into the FEELING of perfect protection, shelter, freedom. Let us really feel in tune with these qualities of Spirit; and they in their turn will attract unto us the ways and means for the home.

PUPIL: So far I have been jumbling everything together in my thought. Should I not take each thing separately and try to enter into the spiritual origin, or purpose, of that one thing before going on to another?

MASTER: By all means finish planting one thought securely in the mind before trying to introduce another. After you have really tuned into the feeling of PROTECTION, SHELTER, SECURITY, FREEDOM, then begin to mentally build your house and people it with a husband and children. Thus you are making a mental picture of the forms you wish the Creative Energy to take. Be **specific** and **accurate** in making your mental picture, remembering that the mental picture you make is the mould into which the un-formed Spirit is poured for solidifying into actual, outward form. The house itself may be a bungalow, or a two-story house, or may be of brick, or stone, or wood, or what not. It may have any number of rooms, doors, windows, a fire-place, etc. In other words you must first **mentally blueprint** your house. When your mental picture is perfectly finished, and your FEELING is that these things ARE yours NOW, and you KNOW that your mind is in perfect tune with the Source of all things, then, and not until then, are you ready to take the next step into the attainment of your desires.

PUPIL: But the matter of the right husband, that seems very difficult for me. First, I am not in the right position to contact men and now I have only two men acquaintances, neither of which I should care to live with in my model home.

MASTER: What you say does not enter into the matter at all. All that the individual does is to place into the Originating Creative Power the QUALITY one wishes to differentiate, just as one plugs into the electric current in the house when one wishes to use it. The light, the heater, the Frigidaire, the fan, the iron, or any other thing one may want to use, all are there. All of the power is already there, too. It is **ready** and **waiting;** all that is necessary is your RECOGNITION of it and your **taking action** to utilize it. Your recognition and your desire cause you to make the right contact; and the power that is there does all the rest. The **ways** and **means** of your meeting the one and only husband are not your own concern; they form themselves into line automatically as a result of your turning on the correct switch.

PUPIL: Do you mean that it is not necessary for me to do anything to try to meet people? Do I not have to go to parties, or visit friends? Sometimes when I should be much happier at home I go to such places, and do such things, because there is always a chance of meeting the right one there.

MASTER: All of that is entirely unnecessary. The power you have turned on within yourself is an ATTRACTING Power, remember! To give you an example: One time when we were in Chicago, living at the Medinah Athletic Club, a young lady came to me with much the same attitude that you express and received the same answer I give here. She was a trained nurse, a graduate of St. Luke's. She was tired of living alone, wished a home, a husband, children. After she had had ten or twelve personal interviews and lessons with me I told her, one morning as she was leaving our apartment, that it would not be necessary for her to come to see me again. She felt sure also that the contact had been made. Our apartment was on the forty-second floor; and as she caught the elevator down she said a "great wave of peace and contentment came over her." In her heart she **had** the **consciousness** of love and protection even now. At the thirty-fourth floor the elevator stopped and a young man who was very ill got into the elevator. Almost at once he folded up on the floor, unconscious. The elevator operator knew him since he had an apartment in the building; and the nurse and operator together got the man back to his apartment, into bed, and sent for the house-physician who said that the nurse had done exactly the right thing. In about an hour the man regained consciousness and sent for his own physician who wished to assign a nurse of his own choosing to the case. But the patient insisted on having the nurse who had helped him from the elevator, and kept her in attendance on him until he was fully recovered. Just about six months later patient and nurse were married.

PUPIL: That was certainly a lucky break for her, that she should take just that elevator, at that time. That seems to me like drawing the lucky number on bank-night at the theatre. Of course someone always wins but there is no certainty about it, is there?

MASTER: Really the two positions are not at all parallel; they are not even similar. With the nurse it was not luck at all. **Deliberately, consciously, in faith,** she had plugged into a circuit of great power within herself, the circuit of Universal Power that we call God, or Life and which did produce a **perfect reciprocity of feeling** and a certain sense of security, protection, provision, companionship. In other words she deliberately "initiated a train of causation directed to her individual purpose," to quote Troward, just as you would attach the cord to your electric- iron if you wished to press clothes. There was no luck in the matter whatsoever; it was purest **science** manifesting, as it always will and does, in answer to a strong desire **scientifically** placed. Whether it is plugging in to a circuit of electric energy or tuning in with the Creative Life Principle the procedure is exactly the same.

PUPIL: I am beginning to see the light. But the case you have just told me about still seems rather spectacular and unusual.

MASTER: That is because you have not trained the objective quality of your mind to know that it can always TRUST the Intelligent Creative Spirit of Life within yourself. You are letting preconceived ideas, and shallow and false ones, take precedent in your mind over pure, scientific **Principle.** You do not feel that you need to know the principles of electricity before you can use your vacuum-cleaner. All we know about electricity is gleaned from what we see it DO. The same thing applies to Life. The innermost principles of Life will always remain a profound mystery.

But one can, and should, live life to the full in the self and love it.

PUPIL: I am wondering if the nurse "lived happily ever after" with her unusually-acquired husband. And did they have the home and the children she so much desired?

MASTER: The couple have lived very happily together for a number of years now and do have a comfortable home and three children. I shall explain more of that later. The secret of living life and loving this: First, your **feeling** towards the livingness of life **in you,** as well as in all life everywhere, should be to RECOGNIZE Life as Intelligent and to know that when this Intelligence is working through you it does not change its essential nature. It has always been a RECEPTIVE Power, that is AMENABLE TO SUGGESTION, and it is **always** RESPONSIVE and CREATIVE. This is the basis of Troward's meaning in his words which I use for my own favorite affirmation, and which, quoted, is this: "My mind IS a center of DIVINE operation. The divine operation is ALWAYS for EXPANSION and fuller EXPRESSION; and this means the **production** of something **beyond** what has gone before, something entirely NEW, not included in past experience though proceeding out of it by an orderly sequence of growth. Therefore since the Divine can not change its inherent nature it must operate in the same manner in me; consequently in my own special world, of which I am the center, it will move forward to produce NEW conditions, always in advance of any that have gone before."

Once you really plug your individual consciousness into the great power of the Universe the above will be your line of thinking. You will involuntarily look to the Life-Principle in you, not only as the only Creative Energy but also as a **directive** Power. That is you will **let** God determine, through your conscious mind, the actual forms and courses which the conditions for its manifestations will always take in your own individual world. Do remember always that the Originating Spirit of Life (of YOUR life, too) is forever a FORMING Power. It is for this reason that we should use such great care in the selection of our HABITUAL thoughts and feelings – for **create they will, and always.**

PUPIL: How may I know, for example, that my true husband is being guided to me, or I to him?

MASTER: By your feeling of CERTAINTY, even though outward conditions show no sign of the fact. Still you are SURE. You feel close. You KNOW you are protected. You feel the influence of love all about you. You have stimulated these special qualities of Life in your individual world by your having persistently looked to God, knowing that He does manifest in you. Your mental attitude of **faith** and **trust** and **expectancy** has attracted all the joys of life. You realize that all that Life has to give is present with you NOW just as all that light has to give is present wherever light is.

PUPIL: Do I understand that if I live as closely as possible in the consciousness of **reciprocity of feeling,** and know that love is guiding, protecting and providing for me with its abundance, I can attract these qualities of life in the form of a man?

MASTER: Yes. For the house and the home FEEL protection, shelter, perfect harmony. For the husband FEEL love and joy; then LIVE IN THE FEELING OF THESE THINGS. **Feeling** is one of the strongest elements in Life and is also the most responsive.

LESSON II: THE FINE ART OF GIVING

PUPIL: It seems to me that the pace you are setting here is going to be rather severe discipline for me. But since it is to be for only a few weeks, if I wish, I shall try it. If there is not a big change for the better, both inside and out, at the end of that time, I can stop. *N'est-ce pas?*

MASTER: Yes, but please do not enter **lightly** upon this study. And do not seek to cultivate an acquaintance with God for the sake of what you will be able **to get from Him.** This is a tragic mistake that many people make, and which is difficult for many of them to rectify. They seek first **to get,** and promise faithfully that they will **then give.** But in so doing they have **inverted the Spirit's Law of Compensation,** which is **good,** which is as **just** as it is good, and which is as **immutable** as it is both good and just.

PUPIL: This sounds interesting. What is this Great Law?

MASTER: The LAW is that FIRST we must GIVE! And **after we have given** the getting automatically follows, just as day naturally comes with the rising of the sun. But the **getting** of anything good **never precedes** the **giving** of something of value! TRUE GIVING, giving with love as unto God Himself, **cannot possibly impoverish anyone;** nor can **withholding** from the Spirit and its service **ever truly enrich one.** Verily, **"'tis more blessed to give than to receive!"** GIVING as unto God opens wide the **Sanctuary of**

Jehovah within us in which we may always find PEACE. GIVING makes of the giver a direct channel for the transmission of Infinite Love and Power into one's daily, hourly life. Then will adversity flee; and **certain achievement** of "all things whatsoever ye will" follows immediately. But, I repeat, **FIRST ye must GIVE!**

PUPIL: But what can we give to God if He already has everything?

MASTER: We can give Him the one thing of which He does not have too much, of which He can never have too much, of which we can never hope to give Him too much. The one thing that God wishes us to give Him, first, last and always, is nothing less than the greatest gift in the Universe. Now what is it?

PUPIL: I am sure that it is Love.

MASTER: Right, but just what is Love?

PUPIL: Why God is Love.

MASTER: That is correct, too. But if God is Love, what is God? And if Love is God, what is Love?

PUPIL: Is this a parable? What is Love? What is God? That's just what I would like to know, too. Tell us please!

MASTER: Just what God is, just what Love is, each person must answer for himself. For after all **your own**

conception of God and of Love IS God and IS Love to you! But perhaps we can set forth a few thoughts that may prove helpful, and which will be practical. To some Love is passion, and can only be conferred upon, or come from, the opposite sex. To some Love is the tenderness of a mother for her child, or of a doting father for his brood. To others Love is the love of friends, parents, or orphans. And there are some who love themselves most of all. But REAL LOVE is Love of God, and for God! To LOVE HIM is the FIRST Commandment! And **if** one keeps this great commandment there is no need of any other commandment; for if we really DO LOVE GOD, which is the first and greatest of the commandments, **we automatically keep inviolate all the others!**

PUPIL: But is it enough to just love God with all of our hearts, all of our souls, and all of our minds? Must we not DO something about it as well?

MASTER: Certainly we must do something about it. **Love without the fruits of Love is dead!** If we love God, we will serve Him devotedly, faithfully, happily, continuously.

PUPIL: How best may we serve Him?

MASTER: BY GIVING OF OURSELVES to our fellowman! By giving of ourselves to our neighbors **as unto ourselves.** A scientist, one like Doctor Walter Reed for example, who gives his very life, and lovingly and gladly, in order to benefit mankind **knows the true love of God.** So does the heroic nurse who ministers to afflicted mankind out of sheer love of mankind. So does the self-effacing, self-sacrificing mother, or father, or teacher, or minister. There are **many ways** in which one may serve. All do not possess scientific talents, nor healing talents, nor comforting talents. But **all do possess something they can give!** Some who feel themselves unable to serve directly give of themselves by donating money to worthy causes, and these, too, are serving God because they Love their neighbors and therefore Love Him. Let me give you an example of TRUE LOVE as I personally knew it in a wonderful woman, one of many cases that I know.

PUPIL: Yes, do give us an example. They always help to clarify things, and show us how others have done what we wish to do.

MASTER: Very well. This divine soul was reared in a home of great wealth and culture. But as a very young woman she made up her mind to go out into the world, "on the firing-line" itself, as she called it, to serve actively lovingly, there. She became a nun, and as such was assigned to a hospital as a trained nurse. As she entered upon her life-work she was filled with love for mankind, with enthusiasm for serving God by serving his suffering ones. And she did serve lovingly, happily, faithfully, tenderly eight hours a day, or even twelve hours daily. But the hospital was woefully understaffed; and Marie, as we shall call her here, was soon subject to call sixteen hours daily; and even during the eight hours when she was supposed to have her rest she was often summoned and asked to serve more. Her quarters were right on the same floor with many of the patients, and this ward was her charge day and night. Often at two or three o'clock in the morning the bell beside her bed would ring with an urgent summons. She would arise at once, go to the patient and minister to his or her wants. But in due time she became physically tired, and of course she began to resent the calls that broke into her rest, especially when it seemed to her, as it often did at these times, that the patient merely wished a drink of water, or wanted a pillow adjusted a certain way, or was merely lonely, all of which were irritating trifles to a weary nurse.

For a month or more these trials went on, seemingly from bad to worse. Marie resolved almost desperately to do something about it, and immediately. So she cast about for a way to best remedy the situation. For days she thought about the matter, asking the Spirit for guidance. At length the flash came, directly from the Infinite! She took up a little card, wrote down the new motto that had been given her, and fastened it on the wall above her bed, right by the service bell, so that she might see it and be again reminded every time the buzzer rang. On the card she had written: "THE MASTER CALLS!" Of course her system worked from the beginning. Quite soon she was saying in immediate answer to the bell, even while sleepily fumbling for her light: "THE MASTER CALLS!" And she would arise and go and serve, without impatience, without resentment, yes, rejoicing in the opportunity to again serve in love. As a consequence her energy was untiring; she easily and joyfully did the work of three nurses, always rested, always fresh, always efficient, always smiling, whenever called. Her patients loved her greatly. She was always cheerful, always encouraging, always aglow, as it were, with a holy Love. And to those who did not know her secret, as very few did, the patients she attended seemed to be "miraculously healed." Let your motto also be: "THE MASTER CALLS!" And remember that the humblest service that you can render to the lowliest of your fellowmen, if rendered in LOVE, **is a direct service to Him!**

PUPIL: This is a profoundly beautiful and powerful illustration. Is that the motto, or the principle, that you use in helping the many who come to you? If not, what is your own personal secret of serving?

MASTER: My own method, in a way, is very similar to that of Marie. Like her I wished to serve lovingly, to serve as many as possible, to help to the limit of my powers in alleviating any and all kinds of suffering, physical, mental, spiritual or other form of unhappiness. Not only do I strive always to help those who seek me out. **Every person** whose hand I take into mine in greeting, **every person** into whose eyes I look, in all places at all times, yes even the shop girl who sells me my hose, the milkman who comes to my door, the beggar on the street, **everyone to whom I speak at any and all times receives the same strong spiritual impulse from me! I INTENTIONALLY SEE THE RADIANT CHRIST IN ALL!**

PUPIL: But I thought that you told me once you **never** mentally treat people unless **they ask for help.**

MASTER: I don't, not specifically, not specifically under any other circumstances. My secret is this: I have **deliberately formed the HABIT of beholding the Christ in every soul that my eyes fall upon!** I do not ever see anyone as being poor, or old, or ill, or bereaved, or lonely, or homely, or evil or imperfect in any way. I BEHOLD EACH AND ALL AS ONLY PERFECT! I SEE ONLY THE RADIANT CHRIST in every one of them BECAUSE THE CHRIST IS in each of them!

LESSON III: THE ART OF RECIPROCITY

MASTER: The Bible, the sages of all time, all sources of real TRUTH, unite in absolute agreement concerning one great thing, namely: That God and Man are ONE and not two, that the "two" are not separated but **indissolubly joined** in perfect and harmonious UNION. The Invisible (Spirit) and the visible (form, or matter) actually ARE inseverably connected. Each is a complement of the other. And the whole of Truth is to be found ONLY in the combination of the "two," which really are not "two" but ONE through ETERNAL UNION!

PUPIL: I am particularly happy about this conclusion because I used to think that a person could not have both **spiritual and physical blessings** at one and the same time. I thought that the physical world had nothing of God in it. Yes, I thought that Spirit was utterly separated from form, or matter. Now I feel sure that the reason I did not make any real progress then was that I was trying to have an **inside** for Life **without an outside,** and an outside without any inside. In other words I was simply living in the physical world without being conscious of the fact that forever I have a direct connection with the Spiritual Realm. I am right, am I not, in believing and **feeling** that I must have the REALIZATION that each is **vitally necessary** to the other for the formation of a Substantial Entity.

MASTER: Yes, you are **exactly right!** No one can go very far on the great highway of Truth until he realizes that there never was, and never will be, an inside to anything without an outside also. While one is visible and the other invisible (to the human eye) the ONLY REALITY **is in the combination of the two.** A **constant awareness** of this fact on our part brings us that radiant realization of ONE-ness, of UNION, that we must have if we hope to make any progress in Truth.

PUPIL: After this one basic realization what other truths must we have?

MASTER: We must KNOW that **underlying the totality of all things is the SOURCE OF ALL THINGS,** the Great Cosmic Intelligence. We must **know** that no physical thing **of itself only** can ever create anything. The physical form is the INSTRUMENT that Life (God) fashioned of His own Essence in order to have something through which He could work His wonders, and give them form also. But He always LIVES in that instrument! Do not ever lose sight of this fact: **The power is always greater than the form** through which it manifests, just as electricity is infinitely greater than the bulb through which it manifests as light. It is through UNION of forms, positive with negative, or masculine with feminine, or Spirit with Soul, that the **creation of all forms,** or channels, or physical things, **results.** This **eternal principle** runs all through the Bible, is the warp and woof of it, the whole substance of it. Seek ye the answer in that Great Book!

PUPIL: But many people say that they Bible is "antiquated," that it is a "book of fables," and of "old wives' tales," etc.

MASTER: How does this concern YOU? Which is the more reliable guide, do you think, the spiritually darkened ones who criticised the Bible or thine own soul which knows light when it sees it? Are you going to do your own thinking or shall you be content to let others do it for you, and wrongly? If we must go to other people in our quest of Truth, let us resolve to go to ones who have the light of the Spirit. For instance, what does Troward say of the Bible? Let his Wisdom be our guide here. He tells us that "the Bible is the Book of the EMANCIPATION OF MAN!" He adds that this means man's COMPLETE "DELIVERANCE from sorrow, sickness, poverty, struggle, uncertainty, from ignorance and limitation, and finally from death itself." This noble conception of Troward's is exactly what the Bible IS. With such a wonderful Book in print one should not be surprised to learn that it has the widest circulation of any book ever published, that it is still the world's best seller. If the Bible were not Truth, it would not live through so many generations and still hold its pre-eminent position. So let us proceed on the assumption that Troward is right, that the Bible DOES contain the secret whereby the art of living a perfectly free and happy life may be attained.

PUPIL: But the Bible has never been a very interesting book to me. I have thought of it as "old world fables."

MASTER: It was uninteresting to you because you did not understand it. Nevertheless it is a most scientific Book, full of interesting facts and life-giving Truth, the finest book ever written about the greatest of all the sciences, the Science of LIFE.

PUPIL: My parents were religious people, church every Sunday morning, prayers every day, and all of that. But I could never see that they were any better off, or any happier – if as happy – than the neighbors who never went to church. But I shall be glad to make an honest effort to understand and follow whatever you outline, even the Bible if you say so.

MASTER: I have spoken. And because you are honest in your desire you will be honest in your thinking; and honest thinking makes a true student. Because you truly wish to understand the art of living you shall come to know it, and when you know Life and really live it you are certain to love it. The Bible IS, I repeat the BOOK OF LIFE, and of Life's immutable Laws. Remember always that **Life's Laws contain within themselves the solution to EVERY human problem!** Indeed "Wisdom is the **beginning** of magic." The Spirit of Christ, or Intelligent Life, within us is the LIGHT of each of us. It will always make the path easy, interesting and joyous IF only we will study and understand how to use our own Divine Power, and THEN REALLY USE IT. Once one has formed the habit of looking to the Bible for the answer to **all** problems it becomes to that one as a lantern carried on a dark night. The next steps ahead may be in total darkness, but when you approach the light you carry illuminates the path and you know exactly where to step, and just what to do. Your **feeling** is influenced in the **right** direction. It is true that the Bible veils its most profound secrets in symbols and parables; but the **Wisdom is there for the earnest and consecrated seeker!** Maybe, the author, was right when he wrote: "The **true** artist finds that the materials for his art are ever present. But the ones **who can discern** the possible uses of these varied materials, and who possess the **instinct, intuition** and **training** to put them to their **best** uses are always few in number. The materials out of which art is made are ever present; but **THE ARTIST appears only at intervals!"** So it is with the mysterious force we call Life. Every person has it; but the ones who understand and use Life's finest possibilities, and who get out of it, consequently, its very richest growth are really very few in number. So let us put into this study of Life our very noblest personal energy.

PUPIL: It seems to me, judging from what you say here and from what you have already taught us in these lessons, that our perfecting of the art of living and loving it is based upon the training of the mind and feeling to the point where we shall find as much joy and satisfaction in **self-discipline** as we formerly found in self-indulgences. Am I right?

MASTER: Yes. Once one has gone that far on the path, he is then around the last turn and on the "way that is straight," **the path of splendor that leads directly to conscious UNION WITH THE FATHER!** The Bible says the art of really LIVING and loving Life centers around the record of man's thoughts and feelings, his aspirations, inspirations and experiences, on his discovery of the Life-Spirit as **"an ever present help in trouble."** When a man has found his REAL SELF (the God-Self, or Christ-Radiance) within, when he has discovered the infinite possibilities and potentialities with which he is forever surrounded, when he LIVES these things and loves the life he lives he becomes the TRUE ARTIST! Then will he use the RIGHT MATERIALS, then will he PRODUCE the RESULTS DESIRED in the form of the picture that he originally conceived!

PUPIL: Suppose one has never had the advantages of higher education, that one's whole life has been common-place and restricted, would such a one be able to understand and apply these beautiful and interesting truths?

MASTER: Yes indeed! One's station in life does not make the slightest difference. Once may be a woman who is trying to cook a good meal in the one and only room that she has, on a one-burner gas-stove. One may be a man who is a shoe-salesman, and who spends his whole time every day trying to satisfy women customers who insist upon his trying to perfectly and comfortably fit dainty shoes to their large feet. One may be a king or queen or a servant or a pauper. High or low, exalted or humble, **man is a spiritual being!** So long as he can **think** he can always change the outer, or physical, effects to suit the desire of his heart. And the very first steps lie **in the thought and in the feeling!**

PUPIL: When one's whole environment is one of poverty, or illness, or other dark limitations, how can one have beautiful and hopeful thoughts? Is it not true that the environment influences one's thoughts and feelings? While one is forced to live in the same adverse environment I do not see how there can be much change.

MASTER: **If** one were perfectly **satisfied** with an environment such as you describe there could not, and would not, be any change. But if one were divinely **dis**-satisfied with such conditions, and very much wished to change them, it may be done any time, as completely as one may wish, by resort to and use of the Laws of Life. Suppose, for example, that you would like a position that is more agreeable, more lucrative, shorter hours, etc. If you go forth to look for such a "job," by all means start out with the feeling that you **have something valuable to GIVE** an employer, and not go out to see how much you can **get.** If you GIVE the getting will automatically follow. Carry the light of God-consciousness with you in seeking betterment of your position; and when you approach your prospective employer **let the light shine.** Suppose too, that you wish a better, more comfortable house in which to live. The **very fact that you desire this change is PROOF POSITIVE that it is for you to have** IF you will meet the requirements. Many persons try to bring harmony into a home by getting a larger and better home, or by changing companions, by moving into another community.

PUPIL: That would help, would it not?

MASTER: **Temporarily** it might. But it would in no sense endure. To attempt to bring happiness or freedom into one's life **through outward changes only** is not wisdom, is not true art. Such is **mis**use of the divine materials. **The change must occur within, and within first!** It must first be established in mind, and firmly enthroned there if it is to be other than only temporarily effective. As long as a **trend of thought** remains the same the result will be the same. The LAW OF LIFE IS: TO CHANGE AN EFFECT THE CAUSE MUST BE CHANGED FIRST. CAUSE LEADS; EFFECTS FOLLOW! THOUGHT IS THE CAUSE; CONDITIONS ARE THE EFFECTS!

PUPIL: Does one's longing for beautiful surroundings, for health and freedom, for a lovely picture in perfect balance, come from the Great Artist who has made all of Nature? Is it He painting His ideal picture for us on the canvas of our individual minds?

MASTER: Yes, God is Mind, Life, Intelligence, Power, Beauty, Love, Harmony, etc. If any of these things are desired by us, and they are, then surely the Creator of them all must have planted that thought-seed in the mind. He must have whispered into that mental ear and that spiritual heart that THE TRUTH IS YOURS! God has chosen YOU as a holy instrument through which to manifest all of His beautiful and wonderful qualities of Life. It is the DIVINE ORDER and WILL that YOU **should manifest that particular thing, that particular place in Life!**

LESSON IV: GOD-CONSCIOUSNESS VERSUS SENSE-CONSCIOUSNESS

PUPIL: Then if our truly fine desires are the desires of God Himself trying to manifest in and through us as individuals, in some particular way, why are there so many misfits in life? Why are there so very few who are doing, really doing, just what they would like to do? Why are there so very, very few living the life they truly wish to live? Why? Why? Why? Surely God can fulfill His own desires.

MASTER: Unless ALL things are possible to God then nothing is possible to Him. God has projected each human forth from Himself, each of us possessing an individual mind, for the **sole purpose** of manifesting Himself and His glory **through us.** Verily the MIND of man IS the SON of God! The Son has been given **absolute liberty.** Each can always make of his life, for a time at least, whatsoever he may choose. Man **already possesses everything that God had to give him!** Each person can make or mar his own picture, exactly as he wishes. By nature man is free to draw from the Ever-Present Parent Mind anything, and all things, that he requires to fulfill his desires. If this is not true then God's highest creation, man, is a mere nothing, an automatic something like a clock which when once wound will run until it runs down. Man IS, however, God's own idea in flesh. The Intelligent Life in man is man's Divine Father! Man is **already perfect and complete,** IS made of the same essence as his Father (God)! There is only one reason why every mortal does not manifest and reproduce the Life, Love and Beauty which we see brought out in such radiance and perfection in all of Nature, manifested in Nature to the extreme point where mechanical and automatic actions can bring them. But we as individuals have a Law of Being that is somewhat different in one way from that which governs the other creatures that are of the world we call Nature. For us that are human the only perfect reproduction of Life, Love, Power and Beauty that we can ever know must come from **Liberty.** That is to say we have **freedom of choice** that is commensurate with that of the Originating Life-Spirit Itself. In other words we as individuals have the LIBERTY of accepting or rejecting either good or evil, **exactly as we may choose** them. And the choice that we make results from **the state of our consciousness.** If we are God-conscious, we ARE gods. But if we are sense-conscious **only,** then we are creatures of darkness, of illness, of poverty, of loneliness, and all other things that are un-desirable. "Choose ye well, therefore, whom ye will serve!" **God-consciousness** or sense-consciousness, which?

PUPIL: You have given us a powerful and illuminating "dose" here. Already we have a whole lesson. But I still do not see why God's highest creation, man should ever reject any of the good things of life.

MASTER: **IF** man **really understood** the **Law of his own Being,** he never should reject the good things. But there are FEW who fully understand this Law, which is a **wide-open door to ABSOLUTE FREEDOM!** Most people believe that the "law of their being" (**purposely** spelled without capital letters) is a **law of limitation** rather than a LAW OF ABSOLUTE LIBERTY! Man "does not expect to find the **starting point** of the Creative Process **reproduced in himself; so he looks to the mechanical side of things for the basis of his reasoning about Life. Consequently his reasoning leads him to the conclusion that Life is limited **because he has assumed limitation as his premise;** and so, logically, he can **not escape from it** (limitation) **in his**

conclusion." Here in this wonderful quotation from Troward you have the WHOLE STORY of limitation. Here Troward shows most clearly that is all a MATTER OF CONSCIOUSNESS! And so the tragedy results because man in his dense ignorance ridicules the idea of TRANSCENDING the law of limitation, forgetting completely (if indeed he ever learned it) that THE LAW can include **all** of the lower laws so fully as to completely swallow them!

PUPIL: From what you say it would seem that man's only reason for knowing limitation of any kind is his own lack of understanding. Is ma to blame because he does not know?

MASTER: No man is to blame for what he does not know. But surely all persons will suffer because of NOT USING WHAT THEY DO KNOW! And they shall keep right on suffering until, like small children, they learn from experience.

PUPIL: It seems "strange," to say the least, that each of us must learn to find his own fuller Life in his own way. Why did not God COMPEL His idea (man) to understand from birth that Life is Joy, and Joy is Freedom, etc.?

MASTER: Please THINK for just a minute! Would there be ANY FREEDOM, ANY LIBERTY, in **that kind** of person? Such an individual should be a mere **automaton** with no sense of LIBERTY at all! God forbid that any of us, His children, become **robots!**

PUPIL: It seems to me that most people feel life is entirely made up of a constant round of prosaic and homely activities which we are obliged to follow: To the shop, or office we go. We toil and slave, and go home again, all worn out and cranky. We sleep, maybe, then arise to repeat it all again for years until in God's mercy we die. There can be no real joy in that kind of life; but to most of mankind that is all. Still this is NOT all, is it?

MASTER: Indeed that is NOT all, not even for the darkest and most limited of persons. However dark, spiritually and materially, a person may be, **deep down in his soul there is a conviction** that **Life holds his desires fulfilled somehow, somewhere, sometime!** He feels also that **IF HE ONLY KNEW HOW** HE COULD FIND A WAY! Some feel that the real joy of LIBERTY can come **only** after putting off the body at death. This is NOT the case, however. EVERYTHING THAT LIFE (GOD) HAS TO GIVE IS HERE IN OUR MIDST, AND RIGHT NOW! As we humans advance in knowledge, either from study or experience, or both, we **overcome** one law of limitation after another BY FINDING THE HIGHER AND GREATER LAW of which **all** lower laws are but PARTIAL expressions. At length we see clearly before us, as our ultimate goal, this Truth: **"Nothing less than the** PERFECT LAW OF LIBERTY – **not** liberty without Law, which is anarchy – but **LIBERTY ACCORDING TO LAW!" When** man learns the Law of his own Being, he will specialize it in all of his ways and will have found his true place. Thus will he bring INTO FORM **all** of the desires of his heart; then will he know the REAL ART OF LIVING!

PUPIL: Can anyone who **will** learn from Life, either by study or experience, that the Creative Energy, with ALL that it has to give, is an Ever-Present, Responsive Quality of Life? Then can one really materialize, really bring into outward form, his most secret and sacred desires! That **would be** the art of living sure enough.

MASTER: THE LAW OF LIFE IS CHANGELESS FOREVER! It is **always** calling to you in these words, or in ones like them:

"Come unto ME! Learn about ME! Through ME ALL things are possible unto you because WE, YOU and I, are eternally ONE! I am LIFE! I am Creative; I am **always Responsive** to the thoughts and emotions with which I am impressed by you! I am MIND! The Law of Mind is MY law! Because this is true it is Truth also that **'AS YOU THINK IN YOUR HEART SO ARE YOU!'** Thinking GIVES FORM to the UN-formed Life!"

PUPIL: This is splendid! But again it is getting "heavy." May we have another personal illustration of the adaptation of this principle to every-day living as people live it? This will help, I am sure.

MASTER: All right; I am always happy to comply with such requests if they will really help you. I once knew a dentist, a very fine dentist and a good man. He confided to me one day that **music** was his very life, and not prosaic dentistry. He said that he was weary of being "down in the mouth all of the time."

"So," I asked, "you feel that you are not in your right place?"

"I **know** that I am not!" he replied.

"Just **why** aren't' you in your right groove?" I queried.

"Because music will not yield me enough money to keep my family in anything like moderate comfort. I feel that marriage and a family are among Life's deepest joys and greatest blessings. But music is like politics; one has to have lots of 'pull' to get into the few places that will really pay for a good violinist."

"Are you **sure** of that?" I asked.

"Yes, quite!"

"Well, Mr. Dentist," I said, "I know a God who is All-Intelligent, All-Powerful, Ever-present, Ever-Responsive and Forever Creative! HE is also the Greatest of Master Artists, the **Real Maestro!** He lives forever deep within your own soul. If you will try going into Him **there,** if you will establish Harmony **there,** and will know and understand the Beauty which your music must express **there,** and if you will be content only with perfection **there** and in your music, I KNOW that you can and will reap all the reward that any one can wish for in music, just as in any other profession, art or business."

"Your words cause my hopes to soar," he said. "But **how** can one like me, one who knows very little about God, contact Him?"

"**Go within yourself!** Go **through,** or beneath, the confusing, bewildering, disheartening past experiences. **Live wholly in and enjoy only the harmonious side of your nature,** which is wise, beautiful and most powerful in all ways. Then practice, practice, practice putting that INNER Beauty and Harmony into vibration through the strings of your violin."

"But I am too old to take this up now."

"Not at all! Loving music as you do, you have kept up with your practice, have you not? Then DO TRY WHAT I HAVE TOLD YOU! Try it with faith and love in your heart.

Hold them there with a determination and pride which simply will not surrender."

The dentist continued to find excuses, many of them, like so many people do, tragically enough. He did not have time, nor did he feel like it, after long, hard days at the office. He should have to give some time to his family, must have some recreation, etc., etc. But I did not hear him. I kept right on singing glowing word-notes for him, tempting him to try hard, inspiring him with courage. **When he stopped finding excuses,** and seemed **really interested,** he asked for the exact method to use. I told him the following steps:

(1) First, he must **thoroughly** make up his mind that his love for music, his deep passion for the expression of harmony was no accident; he must know that **it was nothing less than God Himself** persistently, relentlessly urging **for expression through him.**

(2) He should go carefully over and recite to himself the Lord's prayer, quietly but with much love and feeling, not less than twice every day, each night upon retiring and each morning when he first awakened.

(3) He should faithfully VISUALIZE himself playing, playing, playing, joyfully, harmoniously, enthusiastically playing to large and most appreciative audiences, receiving really handsome checks for his concerts, etc.

(4) After his periods of visualizing he should faithfully use some affirmation that appealed to

him, that would strengthen his faith when it sagged, that would feed his high resolve, that would fan his burning urge to a holy flame.

(5) He should practice, **practice,** PRACTICE his music, striving always with all of his heart and soul to do **much** better with each rendition than he had ever done before.

Within less than one year the dentist **became the** musician! He was making more from his "pot boiler" concerts than he had ever made at dentistry. Within another half-year he began a national concert-tour which within a few months yielded him enough to go to Europe for additional study for two years, and to have his family with him over there. Since that time he has done nothing, professionally, but play his violin. He has not, of course, accumulated a really great fortune, but he and his loved ones have all of the good things of life that they wish, and **this, combined with an abiding sense of happiness, constitutes TRUE WEALTH for any person!**

PUPIL: Does this same plan apply to every one, and the same steps?

MASTER: The SAME PRINCIPLES apply to **all!** The exact plan, and the steps that lead to its fulfillment, will vary a little, of course, with each specific case. But no matter what your big desire may be, your Father's dearest wish for you is the absolute fulfillment of that desire by you, **by you in partnership with Him!** He always LONGS to give you any and all good things! His WHOLE PURPOSE in having created you was that He MIGHT EXPRESS HIMSELF THROUGH YOU! THIS IS **EXACTLY** WHY HE CREATED INDIVIDUALS, and THIS IS WHY HE **DOES LIVE IN** AND **THROUGH** THEM! **If we would** have any of His GIFTS AS OUR VERY OWN we need ONLY to

LIFT UP OUR FALLEN CONSCIOUSNESS TO THIS HOLY BELIEF and THEN **WORK** IN SHEER **JOY** AND **EXPECTATION** towards the LOVELY VISION WE HAVE IN VIEW!

LESSON V: PERSONAL INTIMACY WITH GOD

PUPIL: Please tell me a definite way to get closer to God, to **push** the little love and understanding that I have further into the Great One-ness until my limited vision is completely absorbed in the Unlimited. Will you do this just for me?

MASTER: Gladly. Since this is **your own** book, you may take all the time that you require, and at such intervals as you please, to study it, then study it still some more, and to **practice** it until you have really **mastered** it and made it **a part of your very self.** The very best way **to completely sublimate** your human self, your sense self with all of its limitations, **into the INFINITE is to establish within yourself a** PERSONAL INTIMACY WITH GOD!

PUPIL: But **can** this be done? Do you mean to say that we may actually be on terms of personal intimacy with God, as with a friend or other loved one? Such a thing seems too good to be true, too strange and mysterious to believe.

MASTER: Yes, this can be done. In fact **it is done in each of us at all times** whether or not we are aware of it. Remember always that each of us was made by, and out of the same stuff as, the Ever-Present, Intelligent, Creative Life Itself. Each of us was fashioned out of It Itself; and each of us **IS It Itself in a physical form.** This being so, it automatically follows that each of us is always in a MOST

PERSONAL INTIMACY with God! God **IS** our Maker, our very life, our body, our thoughts, our desires, **our everything!**

PUPIL: Then why are there any troubles at all in this world? Why is not the lot of every person peace, joy and perfection at all times?

MASTER: That question I have answered a number of times, in one form or another. But yet once again let me say that it is all a matter of each individual's own CONSCIOUSNESS. **Our thoughts make us what we are!** The whole shape of our lives, and of what we call "conditions," **take their form FROM OUR MOST HABITUAL THOUGHT AND FEELING!** Don't ever lose sight of this outstandingly important fact.   The Originating Creative Power is **UN**formed relative to your individual life **UNTIL IT FLOWS THROUGH YOUR THOUGHT!** It is through out CONSTANT AWARENESS of the truth that God **IS** ever-resident within us, IS forever flowing through us as thought, that we are lifted right out of the old, limited habits of judging everything from external appearances, or from sense-consciousness only.

PUPIL: But I still do not quite see how this awareness will change the whole life from darkness to light. Just how will it do it?

MASTER: If you are CONSTANTLY AWARE of the fact that **YOU REALLY ARE GOD HIMSELF** in miniature, that you ARE always on terms of personal intimacy with Him as with your own self, **then** you will not any longer think thoughts that are unlike Him. You will not think thoughts of limitation of any nature; you **will not judge anything or anybody** from the standpoint of sense-consciousness. And when you have changed your Thoughts and Feelings to the point where you are **HABITUALLY THINKING ONLY FROM THE SPIRITUAL**

SIDE OF THINGS you will readily discover that to **really KNOW GOD IS TO BE GOD!** Then indeed are you in constant personal intimacy with God; and you will leave far behind you the dismal bogs of failure, lack, disease, loneliness and despair. You will emerge into, **and abide securely in,** the GREEN PASTURES of the fulfillment of your every treasured desire! Persist, persist and yet again **persist,** in your steady recognition of the **Truth** that the **actual purpose** of the Divine in having projected YOU into being from its own Bosom was this and this **ONLY:** That it might CONTINUALLY FLOW THROUGH YOU AS CONSCIOUSNESS, and that it might **always** SPECIALIZE IN YOU AS HEALTH, WEALTH, PEACE AND JOY! Through this realization you lift your thought and feeling above limitations, and this is the solution to every problem. Yes, through the radiant gate of PERSONAL INTIMACY WITH GOD we step into a NEW WORLD in which ALL IS LIFE AND LIBERTY! Truly God **IS** an EVER-PRESENT-EVERYWHERE-ALL-THE-TIME LOVING, RESPONSIVE, CREATIVE POWER!

PUPIL: Since you often encourage us to use the Bible as a standard and a way-shower, can you refer us to a place in the Bible in which we are given a means of establishing this conscious personal intimacy with God?

MASTER: Certainly. The Bible is replete with illustrations of this very principle. For instance, let's turn to St. Matthew, Chapter 22, verses 36, 37, 38, 39 and 40; and note what Jesus, the Greatest of all Great Teachers, says there. Set us study it and analyze it carefully. Here it is:

> (a) Verse 36: "Master, what is the GREAT COMMANDMENT in the Law?" This question, asked of Jesus by the lawyer, was one of **vital importance;** and in the answer that Jesus gave is the GOLDEN KEY that millions desire. **Note** the reply below:

(b) Verses 37 and 38: "Jesus said unto him: "Thou shalt **LOVE** the Lord thy God with **ALL THY HEART,** and with **ALL THY SOUL,** and with **ALL THY MIND!** THIS is the **FIRST** and **GREAT** commandment." Kindly note very carefully, and ponder deeply, the THREE steps that are united into ONE through His use of the word "LOVE." The **heart,** the **soul** and the **mind** constitute **ALL** of the **SPIRITUAL BEING!** Hence if we really love God with **ALL** of our heart and soul and mind, we are in fact loving Him with **ALL OF OUR ALL!** Is this not true? Indeed it **IS!** Here then we have Jesus' **own way,** His **own method,** of establishing within Himself PERSONAL INTIMACY WITH GOD!

(c) Verses 39 and 40 read thus: "And the second (commandment) is like unto it (like unto the first one) Thou shalt **LOVE THY NEIGHBOR AS THYSELF!** On these TWO commandments hang **ALL** the LAW and the prophets." Please observe here the **tremendous importance** that Jesus places upon loving our neighbors as we love our own selves. There are many who pay lip-service to this Divine injunction, and who profess that they really DO love their neighbors as themselves. But when it comes to the crucial test of dividing their possessions in love with a less fortunate neighbor, or of going to any extremity of "trouble" for him, their protestations of love for the neighbors are far too often found to be only mere words, shallow and empty and vain. So **remember this:** in words **WITHOUT DEEDS TO SUPPORT THEM** there is **NO VIRTUE!** It is a FACT that our neighbors (every last one of them) are as precious in the sight of God as we are; in truth our neighbors are an integral part of ourselves, in other forms. It is a FACT also that we can not really love God unless we love our neighbor; and it is a still greater TRUTH that if we DO love our neighbor as we love our self we **are** loving God. God is ONE! Yet most of us make the tragic mistake of thinking that

God is **many,** that our neighbor is one person and we another, etc. The DIVINE REALITY, however, is that ALL PEOPLE (yes every last one of the millions and millions on earth) are ONE BODY UNIFIED FOREVER IN GOD! This being so, it is impossible for us to help a neighbor **(who is our self)** without also helping ourselves. Neither can we criticize, condemn or injure a neighbor **(who is our self)** without doing ourselves greater harm than is done to the neighbor. In PERSONAL INTIMACY WITH GOD there is, in reality NO "neighbor" and NO "self," as two persons, as ones separate and apart from each other; rather each of us is also all other persons, and all other persons are our own selves! When the dwellers on earth learn this all-important lesson that Jesus taught, and when all persons are obedient to this Law, then we shall have the Millennium here in our midst - then will all of us be veritable angels of the ONE DIVINE BODY!

PUPIL: This is a most beautiful and powerful illustration. In addition to studying about it and thinking about it what else should we do about it?

MASTER: The most important thing of all is to PRACTICE it, to LIVE it! Otherwise there is no virtue in it at all. If you can accept these words of Jesus as Truth, then ALLY yourself with them in your THOUGHT and FEELING and ACTIONS, then will your whole being be fed with spiritual MANNA. You will be given constant suggestions by the Spirit regarding the sanest and most fruitful methods of living your own personal life in TRUE UNITY WITH GOD.

PUPIL: And will this not develop still more in us that great essential to which you gave such importance in Lesson Number One, namely a **good disposition?**

MASTER: Indeed it will! And no age in all of history has ever more needed to learn and practice this great lesson of GROWTH, DEVELOPMENT and true ENRICHMENT than the people of today. Many read the Truth; **few assimilate it!** Many hear the Truth; **few heed it!** Many know the Truth; FEW DO IT! That is exactly why there is a real MASTER only at long and rare intervals. The price of MASTERY is really easy; but it is so much contrary to sense-consciousness (out of which all selfishness is born) that FEW have the courage, the faith and the spiritual stamina, and the LOVE, to try it earnestly, or to stick to it through outward confusion, until it HAS BEEN PROVED!

PUPIL: Is there any other method you can think of that will help us to understand this Great Law still better? Are there any short cuts? In the study I mean, not in the practice of it?

MASTER: Yes, there are short-cuts from which a **truly observant** and intelligent person may find this Law actually fulfilled in beautiful harmony, and from which we humans may learn a very great deal, **if** we will. Perhaps the greatest of these short-cuts to ILLUMINATION is the one that is most widely distributed, and to which every last soul has access in one form or another, and with very little "trouble" if they sincerely wish to seek it out. I mean NATURE, of course. **ALL** of Nature shows forth the GLORY OF LIVING IN CONSTANT PERSONAL INTIMACY WITH GOD!

By way of example of what I mean, let us briefly study the four seasons of the year, and the reaction of Nature to each. Spring in all of Nature is the period of IMMORTALITY expressed anew, and in wonderful splendor! It is the season of **budding,** of **flowering,** of **mating,** of **Generation** and of **Re-generation,** all of which are among the HOLIEST of the functions of Nature. And **mark well** how **all** of Dame Nature's children are always **OBEDIENT** to the urge of Spring, to the sublime song of the Spirit! **Only men** are **rebellious** to the holy commands of the Spirit; and it appears quite obvious that **only men sin.** How long will it be before we who are human awaken to the TRUE GLORY that **is** OUR DIVINE BIRTHRIGHT?

In the realm of Nature **summer** is the time when **fruits** are formed, developed and ripened in fulfillment of the Law of the Spirit. It is the season when seeds are formed within the fruits so that with the coming of another spring all of Nature may obey again the great injunction found so often in the account of Creation in Genesis, namely; "Be ye fruitful and multiply, and fill the face of the earth with fruit."

With the **autumn** comes the PRECIOUS HARVEST, the time when the radiant PROMISE that was given in the spring is FULFILLED IN FORM, just as every promise of the Spirit to **US** will surely be **manifested in form in our lives,** and with a **most bountiful harvest, IF** only we humans will learn to **OBEY** the Spirit without question, as do the fair children of Nature, and cease our foolish rebellion that is the **one and only source of all** of our afflictions!

Then follows the **winter** and Nature RESTS from its labors of the spring, summer and fall, just as we also must have our periods of rest. But winter positively is **NOT** aging, or decadence, or death, not in Nature. It is the season of rest, of slumber, **only.** But if you want to think that winter is the symbol of "death," as some people insist upon doing, I will agree with you for a minute solely for the purpose of pointing out the **FALLACY** of death, or the belief in death, as clearly revealed by Nature. In winter Nature does **APPEAR** dead. **BUT IS IT DEAD?** By no means! With the first few warm days of spring the **LIFE** which has been merely SOMNOLENT in Nature, (but which has NOT perished because it can NOT perish, **not ever)** again **RESPONDS!** The buds, animated anew by the vitality of the Spirit, swell and burst; and the leaves and flowers that were HIDDEN from view (but THERE nevertheless) come harmoniously, joyously forth in their beauty and glory to express IMMORTALITY! As Nature DOES so may MAN DO ALSO if he only will. IF YOU WOULD KNOW TRUE ILLUMINATION, and the POWER and the GLORY that are born of it, GO THOU TO NATURE! STUDY HER WAYS AND BE WISE! STUDY HER WAYS AND **REALLY LIVE!**

LESSON VI: INDIVIDUALITY
(What Is the Truth about the Individual and His Individuality?)

MASTER: Have you ever given thought to the matter of HOW you came into existence? Are you convinced that there was, and is, a DEFINITE PURPOSE in the Divine Mind to account for your being here on earth? Or do you think that you create the purpose of your life for yourself, independently of all other factors, after you come into this world?

PUPIL: You ask questions that I scarcely know how to answer. These questions have perhaps been of mild and brief interest to me in the past; but I have never given them any real thought. I have let my mind wander as concerns these points. One time I would think that the Creative Parent Mind does have a definite purpose in my being here, and that this being so there is no use in my trying to change things. But it would then occur to me that this conception of things would mean the "pre-destination" of the fundamentalists. So I would change my mind and decide that I must have some hand in determining my mental and spiritual progress. Is this right?

MASTER: Indeed you do have a hand in your self-development. You have a VERY GREAT PART in it! The life that is you as an individual came directly out of the Great

Whole of Intelligent Life (God), from out of its very own sacred heart-center. Your very life is the Spirit's GIFT OF ITS OWN SELF TO YOU! Secondly, the Divine DID have a specific purpose in having made you namely: That it might have a NEW FORM, a new center, through which it might operate as THOUGHT and FEELING, and through which it might yet more fully ENJOY IT-SELF in a particular way. This also is the Spirit's GIFT OF ITS OWN SELF TO YOU! **BUT** the manner in which you as an individual use these HOLY GIFTS is left entirely in your hands, without interference from the Spirit. You were given other holy boons; you were given INITIATIVE and SELECTION; you were given **absolute** FREEDOM OF CHOICE! The distance that you travel towards the goal of spiritual perfection in this earth life **depends solely upon YOU,** just as the degree of rapidity with which you may mentally grow is entirely up to **YOU!**

PUPIL: But are we not given certain divine urges, or longings at all stages of our lives which will help us to know the right way to go? Are we not given these certain desires, or impulses, or stimuli?

MASTER: Certainly. And unless one follows these Divine impulses one is never really quite satisfied, one is always restless, always feels that some essential is lacking, that his right place eludes him. Your very individuality is an EXACT COMPLEMENT of the Great Whole, is a specialized action of all of Life. The only difference in the Life, the Love, the Beauty or the Power of the Universal (God) and of the individual (man), as expressed through the Universal and the individual, is a difference in SCALE. **THE QUALITY** OF THE TWO (which in reality are but ONE) **IS EXACTLY The SAME!** The very same Creator who made and directs the whole universe also made and will direct you, **if you will let Him do so,** because HE HIMSELF LIVES IN YOU as the Life of you. His infinite Creative Power and Intelligent Love are the VERY SAME IN YOU that they are in all other created things. Therefore it is not just sentiment to **say** and **feel** and

KNOW, as did Jesus: **"THE FATHER** (God) **AND I ARE ONE!** THE FATHER **IN** ME, HE DOETH THE WORK!"** If only we will develop a **constant recognition** of this most profound Truth, we shall then really HAVE an **abiding** sense of LIBERTY, of LIBERTY IN UNION, of **LIBERTY IN CONSCIOUS UNION WITH ALL OF LIFE!** This is not just an idle but beautiful rhapsody; it is a simple, but most powerful and illuminating, STATEMENT OF FACT!

PUPIL: Am I right then in believing that if I could really think myself into an unshakeable conviction that God IS ever-present in me, and that ALL of His Creative Power is MINE to draw from at my own will and pleasure, I could accomplish ANYTHING and EVERYTHING that I might wish, and could BE and HAVE whatsoever I might desire?

MASTER: Yes, you are right. The Creative Power of God in us is UNformed with respect to what we may wish to accomplish until **we ourselves give it definite direction with our thought and feeling.** It is ALWAYS RESPONSIVE, remember, to any and all of our thoughts and feelings. These things being true, and they ARE true, any person may **BE, DO** and **HAVE** whatsoever that one may desire, **IF,** of course, one **ACTIVELY WORKS** in a corresponding direction. It is logic, it is purest gospel, that there is **no other way** than the one that **Life's true purpose in us is to be forever seeking to express itself through us as FREEDOM!** Remember always, I urge you, that our THOUGHTS and FEELINGS DO BECOME THINGS, and that they determine the shape that the unformed substance of the Spirit takes in its **living expression** in our individual lives. It is, as Troward says, like water flowing through a pipe; the water **always** assumes the shape and the size of the pipe through which it is sent. It is like harnessed electricity which **always** manifests in exact correspondence with the kind of instrument through which it passes as it works. It the light-bulb the electricity ACTUALLY BECOMES light; in the door-bell it rings the bell; in the refrigerator it generates cold; in the stove it becomes heat. It is the same electricity, the same Power, in every case; and the **instrument through which it passes determines what the Power is and what it does!** Once a person truly grasps the real meaning of the Spirit's Principles, then one realizes fully that we as individuals are actually sent out from the very Heart of God Himself in order that we may BECOME and BE new and perfect centers through which HE can operate in **JOY,** in ever-increasing **JOY.** This and **this only, is the will of God towards us!** Yes, the exalted mission of each of us is that we may be new instruments for DIVINE EXPRESSION. If we **will** to become that, and will make the necessary mental and physical effort to realize this Truth, then we will KNOW that we ARE filling our right place in life. We shall experience true and lasting happiness then because we SHALL BE DOING the things we MOST ENJOY DOING. There will be an ever present-sense of GROWTH in our lives also. Only a very few individuals have ever reached this empyrean height in consciousness while on the earth-plane; STILL IT IS POSSIBLE TO ALL. Because so few attain this exalted level most people have the merest existence, one that is filled with seemingly continual and perplexing problems of one sort or another.

PUPIL: It seems to me there are many more people who are unhappy here than happy ones. So many of my personal friends feel themselves to be misfits in life, I do not think that I know even one person, including myself, who is perfectly happy. If one has health, as some do, then that one may have financial troubles. If they do not have financial worries, and no real physical woes, then they have family discord. And so on it goes until one wonders if there is such a thing as complete happiness in this phase of existence.

MASTER: You are right; and the **real** reason for all of this unrest is this: These individuals have not **recognized** that their THOUGHTS and FEELINGS are the ONLY

INSTRUMENTS by which the All-Creative Energy **CAN** manifest in their lives. It is of no avail to blame Providence, or other people, for your troubles. No matter what form chaotic conditions take in your life YOU ALONE ARE RESPONSIBLE FOR THEM; and YOU ALONE CAN RECTIFY THEM through **use** of your inseverable contact with God. Once one learns through study and practice, or through experience, TO ALLOW the WILL OF GOD (which is always GOOD) TO HAVE FREE ACTION IN AND THROUGH HIM, **then** ALL BONDAGE TO CONDITIONS IS OVER!

PUPIL: At the risk of appearing dull may I ask yet again just how this can be done by each of us?

MASTER: I have given you the answer a number of times in this book; but it is worth repeating in a little different form, for it is an ALL-IMPORTANT item. Here is the answer yet again:

(1) Mentally go deep within your inmost self, your own Divine inmost, and ask yourself: "What DOES God really meant to me?" "What must the Divine Nature in me be like?"

(2) Once you have formed a **definite** and **positive** conclusion on these points, try to **reproduce this same feeling all through your whole being.** KEEP TRYING, and you will succeed in doing it. It is worth the effort required, a million times over.

(3) Do NOT let yourself be discouraged with this practice if you do not seem to get immediate results. Remember always that Troward says "**it is**

the intention that counts; it is the intention which registers on the reproductive disk of Creative Life."

(4) Another powerful help, to me personally at least, is to diligently use that affirmation from Troward which begins: **"My mind IS a center of Divine operation,"** etc. (See "Your Invisible Power," or Troward's "Dore Lectures"). The Lord's Prayer is also an excellent aid, as I have repeatedly written herein.

(5) Try, try, try with **all** of your concentrated purpose to LIVE HOURLY in the FEELING of the affirmation, or the prayer. Do NOT let yourself slip and fall by indulgence in what you may call "justifiable impatience" for there is no such thing. Anger, or jealousy, or fear, and all like things, will cause you to slip also, for these things are unlike your idea of God, or of God's thought.

PUPIL: That is a **very** tall order!

MASTER: Not when you realize constantly that it is the **intention that counts.** The more you keep your **intention** right the less frequently will you slip in your practice of these principles; and soon your whole life shall have been altered until it **IS** like your own conception of God.

PUPIL: Many people who **seem** to have a very good idea of Christian Science, Divine Science, Unity, etc., try very hard for more money, better health, higher social position. Yet they do not seem to get far. Why?

MASTER: Whether or not they are conscious of it they are looking to the **outside** as the source from which these things shall come to them. But the ORIGIN OF ALL GOOD THINGS IS WITHIN! All good is WITHIN your own Life-Stream; and this MUST BE RECOGNIZED! Our recognition of the WITHIN, the Spiritual, as the TRUE SOURCE of all good things WILL GIVE THEM FORM in the OUTER or physical, WORLD in which we live. Once the contact is made WITHIN, and faithfully held, the **things** will AUTOMATICALLY come to pass in the outer. The whole secret is this: We MUST know exactly **WHO** we are, **WHAT** we are and **WHY** we are! Knowing this, our contact with the SOURCE OF ALL GOOD is never interrupted. It is our task to take care of the INNER things; and if we do, the outer things SHALL TAKE CARE OF THEMSELVES. THEN SHALL WE FO FORWARD, AND ONLY FORWARD, HAPPILY, HARMONIOUSLY, SERENELY ACCOMPLISHING ANY AND ALL GOOD THINGS THAT WE MAY WISH!

LESSON VII: PERSONAL POINTERS ON SUCCESS

MASTER: No one ever slides into real success without personal effort. It **takes all one has** to attain unto real success, and to hold it: but by the very same law each person **HAS ALL IT TAKES!** If we are willing to reach out for achievement, and to use all of our faculties to that end, then unqualified, constant success is surely ours. It has been said that Napoleon never blundered into a victory. He always won his battles IN HIS MIND before he won them on the field. **This is exactly what every successful person does!**

PUPIL: What is the very first step on the high road to success?

MASTER: The very first step is to **DECIDE definitely and positively what form of success you want.** Henry Ford, for example, wished with all of his heart and soul to make BETTER AUTOMOBILES CHEAPER, cars that were within the financial reach of **all** persons. Thomas A. Edison wanted to provide various efficient electrical appliances at moderate prices for the convenience and comfort of the **world.** Jesus the Christ had one outstanding desire ever-present in His consciousness: To SHOW THE WAY for every human being to find the Father-Principle within himself, to show all how to **find** and **know** and **trust** that Infinite Divine Power which really will, and DOES, protect all, guide all, provide for all. Each of these men had a divine urge that burned within him, an all-consuming passion to do **one** thing better than it may have been done before. Because they KNEW EXACTLY WHAT THEY MOST WISHED TO DO THEY DID IT!

PUPIL: If one does not know exactly what line of endeavor to pursue, what is a good thing to look for in determining just what is best to do?

MASTER: Here is another most-important essential to success; this will give you your cue. The MORE GOOD a person CAN DO FOR OTHERS with his product, his life, his work, or whatever it may be, the GREATER SUCCESS will that person **have!** No one ever succeeded in any very great degree whose dominant motive was that of personal gain **only.** If one actually helps others, many others, to live happier, better, more successful lives, one need give little thought to the gain that will accompany the success; for **if** one does this the gain to self can not possibly be withheld. One's chief motive then in reaching out for success is not to see how much he may help himself but to see how greatly he may help many others.

PUPIL: These two steps are most helpful to me. But before taking other steps may I ask just what pitfalls I should look out for most when first I start on the road?

MASTER: Here are two of the most common snares, I think:

(1) Never yet has success come, and never shall it come, to any person who simply wishes for it. Mere wishes are idle and utterly impotent unless the wish is great enough to INSPIRE ONE TO IMMEDIATE ACTION. Yes, ACTION, not wishes, is the BIG THING.

(2) Keeping your mind centered on the big success that you **"are going to be"** will NEVER bring it to pass. You must KNOW yourself **successful** NOW. So long as one looks upon success as a FUTURE acquirement just so long will success be POSTPONED, just so long will its attainment always remain FUTURE. From the very start one must learn to BACK UP the THOUGHT with the FEELING, the absolute conviction, that **I AM SUCCESS NOW!**

PUPIL: These are splendid, too. Now I am ready for another step forward.

MASTER: Since you have now firmly resolved to make a business of acquiring true success in accordance with Life's immutable Laws, you must **throw your whole energy** into making your mind a center for **positive thoughts only,** for **constructive thoughts only.** You are **deliberately** careful of the words you use. You are **deliberately** careful of your mental reaction to the words you may hear. For instance, if you hear people talking about a tornado you should **not** let your thoughts dwell upon destruction but rather upon **tremendous power POSITIVELY used.** If you hear people talking about disease, you should inwardly know that while disease is a natural result of broken natural laws it is not necessarily evil, and that in Life as Life ALL IS GOOD AND PERFECT. In a word it will be necessary for you to avoid all detours, even though they may **appear** easy and short.

PUPIL: What are some of these detours? How will they be marked?

MASTER: All of them should be marked with lots of red lanterns for certainly they are dangerous to one seeking success. Here are a few of them which you will recognize as questions that you have asked yourself, just as millions of other Truth-seekers; and yet they wonder why success always eludes them.

(1) "Well, WHY doesn't it come?"

(2) "WHEN will it come?"

(3) "MAYBE **this** is the way it will come."

(4) "Perhaps it is not God's will that I have this."

Success does not come for the one who asks: "Well, why doesn't it come?" simply because he is asking WHY rather than KNOWING that IT NOW IS! For the one who whimpers: "When will it come?" it shall never come so long as he asks WHEN. What they wish NOW IS or else it never will be. And as concerns "God's will" for us His will for us is **anything good we may desire.**

PUPIL: Just why is it that if we wish success for ourselves only, for personal gain only, we shall not be apt to get it?

MASTER: Here is an illustration. Suppose you went to your own personal banker and asked him for a loan of one hundred thousand dollars, knowing that he had that much, and more to loan and that your worth justified a loan of that amount. No doubt his first question would be that one that bankers always ask first of anybody seeking a loan, i.e., "What do you want the money for?" Let's suppose you answered: "Oh, I wish to take a year's cruise on my yacht, doing nothing, just loafing, resting, sleeping; eating. I need the change, you see." Do you think he would let you have the money? **No** not a soul! No more will the Great Universal Banker (God) under like, or similar, circumstances. You must approach Him with a really good idea, one which will bring good to many, not just to yourself. I know men who have millions and who began with **no** money, who began **only with an idea.** Their basic ideas were so **universal** towards the **production of good** they were able to secure from others all the money necessary to finance the beginning of their enterprises. The great secret of **individual** success is the very same as that of the **national** success that has made America the wealthiest land on earth, and is **this:** Our men of affairs, of greatest success, have learned to **share with all** of our people **through benefiting all** of the people, either directly or indirectly, through **dispensing higher quality goods at less cost,** through sharing earnings more generously with employees, etc. They have learned that it is an **absolute science** that **giving to and sharing with many always have getting as a natural correlative!** Get your thought right; capture an idea that will prove helpful to many; then DRAW IN CONFIDENCE on the Unlimited Banker for all that you require. You will discover that you can not keep money from gravitating to you. Herein lies SURE and CONTINUING SUCCESS!

PUPIL: May we have here, in conclusion, the gist of this whole matter of true success, in summary form? This will facilitate ready reference by us who are students.

MASTER: Certainly you may have this. It may be said that the steps to success are seven in number; and here they are:

(1) **Thoroughly** make up your mind **exactly** what you want most right now.

(2) Be **certain** that your desire has in it the element of good for many. Then ask your own inmost soul for the most perfect idea, or ideas, relative to your desire, ideas that will PRODUCE GOOD FOR MANY.

(3) Make a mental picture of your desire as **FULFILLED NOW,** and NOW only, making the mental picture **complete, vivid, alive with feeling.** This is the meaning of Jesus' great statement to **"ASK BELIEVING THAT YOU (ALREADY) HAVE."** In the mental picture you ACTUALLY DO HAVE (mentally, which is the realm of all TRUE CAUSATION) your desire right now. Once you really get into the FEELING that what you want **already IS yours** (mentally) you will SOON realize how quickly it grows into **actual FORM.** Keep out of your mind all fear-habits of thought. Know that fear-habits can be readily changed into FAITH-HABITS. Year and faith are the same, one being one end of the stick and the other the other end of the same stick. The fear-end of the stick is a SHOVEL and will surely dig the grave of success; the FAITH-end is a JEWELLED CROWN ready to adorn the head of any who will wear it.

(4) If necessary, **COMPEL** yourself to **implicitly believe** that the same Power that give you your desire in the beginning will also GIVE YOU THE WAYS AND MEANS OF ITS TRIUMPHANT FULFILLMENT.

(5) Meditate carefully at frequent intervals on the REAL PURPOSE of your desire. This REAL PURPOSE of the desire, or the thing, is the ALL-IMPORTANT SPIRITUAL PROTOTYPE for the thing you want. Also go over the Lord's Prayer **very** carefully several times daily. It will help you much in meditating more profoundly, and will TUNE YOUR MIND IN WITH THE POWER (GOD).

(6) Every night before going to sleep, and every morning upon first awakening, make a solemn vow to live CLOSE to your God every conscious hour, to

see **only** good in all, to entertain only good and constructive thoughts about everything and everyone.

(7) Frequently mentally see yourself ALREADY ENJOYING YOUR **FULFILLED** DESIRE. Do this every time you think of the desire; and especially at night and morning, just before sleeping and at once upon awakening, for at these periods the subconscious element of mind is **especially** amenable to suggestions. In this way you DO ALREADY HAVE your desire perfectly fulfilled (mentally); and if you **persist** in it you shall surely have it soon in its physical form right in the midst of your life. For example, the great bridge that now spans the Golden Gate at San Francisco was **first** pictured **COMPLETED** and **IN USE** by many in the MIND of its designer before it became an actual reality. But **by** mentally picturing the bridge as ALREADY COMPLETED and SERVING MANY PEOPLE WELL the designer DREW from the WHOLE UNIVERSE the power necessary to have it actually built.

These SEVEN points are the keys, or steps, to the attainment of real success in **any line** of endeavor. MARK THEM WELL, and **above all other things USE THEM!** They are TRUTH! **THEY WORK!**

LESSON VIII: INSTANTANEOUS HEALING

MASTER: It seems strange to one who has made real progress along God's great highway of Truth just how many mortals who are on the same journey will make detours that are altogether unnecessary, or will even turn and go in the opposite direction from their desired goal. For example, nearly everyone, it seems, is very much interested in a newly discovered disease, or in just disease as such, while the thing that all of us wish to know most about is PERFECT HEALTH and how to reach that rich experience that is spoken of in the Apocrypha, Ecc. 30:15-16, which reads: "Health and a good estate of body are above all gold: and a strong body above infinite wealth!" Of course we all know that it is impossible to find the Truth about HEALTH by **holding our interest and attention on disease.**

PUPIL: But we know that there is disease. Must we not reckon with this fact?

MASTER: One who recognizes disease as a reality has thus made his own law about it, and for him disease is inevitable. If disease is what you **think** and **believe** then disease is a fact **for you.** All bodily inharmony is **first** a thought and a belief; consequently its CURE is from the **mental side** also. It has been said that "the Absolute (Spirit) is like the air which carries odors, both good and bad, but which remains forever untainted by them." In the Absolute all is health and harmony; it may carry the beliefs of mortals in disease about with it yet it is never tainted by them!

PUPIL: But since the belief in disease is so widely prevalent is it not well for us to know how to handle disease, or belief in disease, from the spiritual standpoint?

MASTER: It would be more scientific to know how to handle HEALTH; and we shall devote this lesson to Healing, to living in conscious harmony with Life's laws. We shall start with the fine art of giving an **effective** spiritual treatment, or mental treatment. There are a number of most important points for the healer, or practitioner, to always remember and **always practice** in this respect.

PUPIL: Which point is the most important of them all?

MASTER: That is difficult to answer since all of them are vitally important; but one of them is this: The practitioner should have firmly fixed in mind the FACT that there is but ONE MIND and but ONE EXPRESSION of this one Mind although it fills all space with its numberless manifestations. This awareness removes the line of demarcation between patient and healer. Another vital essential is this: If one hopes to be of any help to a patient one must NOT give treatment **for disease.** That would surely INTENSIFY the disease! In giving a spiritual treatment the practitioner should utterly dismiss all thoughts of disease and of personality from the mind. To hold the thought on disease would mean MORE disease. Rather the healer should mentally see Life WHOLE, FREE, AT PEACE and IN HARMONY through the power of the Radiant Christ within.

PUPIL: But suppose the patient is right there in front of you at the time of the treatment, that he is ill and in great pain. How can the practitioner avoid seeing the ill condition?

MASTER: If one is not sufficiently disciplined in mind to see through, or beyond, the **condition** one should not attempt to be a healer; or else such a one should confine his efforts **exclusively to absent mental treatments.** To see, or to believe in, any **condition** that a patient may seem to have disarms a practitioner immediately and renders his efforts impotent in behalf of the patient.

PUPIL: Are the absent mental treatments always just as effective as ones given face to face? Does not the distance of the patient from the source of treatment raise a barrier to the effectiveness of the treatments?

MASTER: A well trained and experienced practitioner is able to treat just as effectively absently as presently; and there are some who do better work absently. In Spirit there is neither TIME nor SPACE, and the distance of the patient from the healer makes no difference at all. You see the first mental step that the practitioner takes is that of clearing his or her mind of the presence of anything except the ONE GOD-SPIRIT. Thought is unbelievably fast in its transmission and **can span the earth instantly;** and it does not **lose any of its power in the transmission!** In giving an absent treatment the healer should be POSITIVE that the thought sent forth reaches the recipient NOW and with INFINITE POWER.

PUPIL: Why is it so vitally important to know that the Truth for the patient is his **now?** If he is ill it does not seem quite reasonable to me that he could be made whole right now.

MASTER: Nevertheless it is either now or never! In the Absolute the ONLY time there is the ETERNAL NOW. To it there is **no past;** nor is there any future. To it there is ONLY the PRESENT. If the practitioner holds the thought that the patient "will be all right," it will **always** be **"will be"** for the patient because the healer is POSTPONING the healing until some future time, and there is no future known to the Spirit, as I have said. Did Jesus ever say to any of those who were healed by Him: "You will be healed. Arise and go"? No, not ever. Always He spoke to them in the PRESENT tense; always He told them something to this effect: "You **ARE** WHOLE! Go in Peace!"

PUPIL: Just what are the mechanics of giving a mental treatment for one who is present personally with the practitioner?

MASTER: The steps in giving a **successful** mental treatment under such circumstances are these:

(1) Have the patient RELAX physically as completely as possible, **all over,** toes, ankles, knees, spine, shoulders, arms, hands and even the **eye-lids** (for the eyes should be closed in the silence). The whole body of the patient should be as limp as possible. The greater the physical relaxation you may induce on the part of the patient the greater his RECEPTIVITY to the mental treatment will be.

(2) Have the patient "empty" his **conscious** mind as completely as is possible, trying to think of nothing at all insofar as this can be done; have him try to make a vacuum of his mind, as it were. This complete RELAXATION of the conscious mind also induces a much greater RECEPTIVITY.

(3) The healer **MUST completely remove the line of demarcation between the patient and self.**

There are not two persons present, not really, not patient and practitioner. The two are ONE, and the establishment of this FACT firmly in the mind of the healer is of **untold importance.** REMEMBER that **Mrs. Jones,** practitioner, is NOT giving **Mrs. Smith,** patient, a mental treatment. As long as the one treating is aware of any sense of separation, or distinction, between patient and self there will be little if any results achieved.

(4) Once all sense of separation is really removed from the practitioner's consciousness, the actual treatment is given. The patient is now in a **passive,** or **receptive** attitude, both mentally and physically. The healer is in an **active,** or **generating,** position. Yet the "two" are **one,** the one person being the **negative** pole, the other the **positive,** and between them the healing current of Life may now freely pass. Into the **Absolute** the practitioner now projects a steady stream of **positive, constructive, powerful thought-energy,** at the beginning of which process the patient's name is either silently or audibly called in order that the flow of Spirit may be given DEFINITE DIRECTION. The receptive attitude of the patient picks up the flow of power and so it is made his own. The affirmation the healer uses at the beginning of the silence may be said aloud once or twice although this is not necessary. Into the Bosom of the Spirit, into the Fruitful Silence, the practitioner thinks and dwells with **intense concentration and feeling,** yet without any sense of strain whatsoever.

PUPIL: Upon what thought does the healer dwell in the silence?

MASTER: Upon the SPIRITUAL PROTOTYPE for the organ that may seem to be diseased, or for the thing or condition that may be desired. This SPIRITUAL PROTOTYPE is yet another thing that is of VITAL importance. To dwell in thought upon anything **physical,** anything which has form, is to be on the plane of LIMITATION, of SECONDARY CAUSATION, of EFFECT. BUT to think steadily upon the SPIRITUAL PROTOTYPE is to MENTALLY **BE** in the realm of the ABSOLUTE which is the INFINITE, which is **FIRST** CAUSE or PRIMARY CAUSATION, which is the CAUSE ITSELF and NOT the effect.

PUPIL: To me this spiritual prototype, important though I am sure it is, is the hardest thing in all of this study "to get hold of" mentally, the most difficult point to really understand. May I have some helpful pointers on this matter?

MASTER: That is true of many, in fact for nearly all "beginners" in this study. Perhaps the spiritual prototype is difficult for you because it is **FORMLESS.** Then, too, it may seem hard to understand because it is a new idea to you, one with which you are unfamiliar, of which you are not accustomed to thinking. Yet it is quite SIMPLE, once you know its nature. Here are some good rules to follow in this matter:

(1) The spiritual prototype of anything is the **thing itself in its most incipient state,** is the **actual origin** of the thing in the Universal Mind.

(2) To find the spiritual prototype for anything it is only necessary to determine in your own mind the **PURPOSE** of the thing, whatever it may be. This is an INFALLIBLE rule. Suppose, for example, one wished a good automobile and would like to

know the spiritual prototype for it. One would mentally ask: "Exactly what is the PURPOSE of an automobile? What is it for? What does it do? What do I really want with a car" The automobile is, of course, an instrument, a means of **PROGRESS,** of rapid, pleasant, harmonious PROGRESS. This being so, then the spiritual prototype for an automobile is **PROGRESS.** At least this is what a car means to **me;** but in selecting a spiritual prototype for anything each one should **think out for himself** just what the PURPOSE of the thing is **TO YOU.**

JOE VITALE

LESSON IX: INSTANTANEOUS HEALING
Continued

PUPIL: Will you please give us a few other prototypes, and show as how they are arrived at? With still a few more examples to serve as guides, I am sure that I shall then know how to form my own prototypes for any particular thing desired or required.

MASTER: Very well; here are a few more. Let us take the head, for example, supposing that one had a belief in a violent headache. The head is the house of the brain; and the brain is the **instrument of** the mind, but in no sense the mind itself. What is the **purpose of** the mind? It is TO KNOW, TO KNOW GOD, the CAPACITY TO KNOW GOD! Can a CAPACITY TO KNOW ever really ache, or hurt, it being a FORMLESS THING? No it can **not!** The spiritual prototype for the head then, as I see it, is the CAPACITY TO KNOW GOD. Now for a minute let us consider the eyes. What is the **purpose of** the physical eye? It is the **instrument of DISCERNMENT,** which is a purely spiritual factor, DISCERNMENT as such having no form of its own. The CAPACITY OF DISCERNMENT is the spiritual prototype for the eyes, to **me.** Here are a few other spiritual prototypes for you; and in these that now follow I shall not explain for you just how I arrived at the conclusion. I shall name the particular organ, or part, of the body and the prototype for it, as I see it, and give you the benefit of thinking out for your self just why I have chosen this particular prototype for each specific thing.

TEETH — Capacity to analyze and dissect God's ideas;

LUNGS — Capacity to KNOW LIFE as LIFE;

HEART — Capacity of LOVE;

STOMACH — Capacity of UNDERSTANDING;

LIVER — Capacity of FAITH;

KIDNEYS — Capacity of PURITY and CLEANLINESS.

The spiritual prototype, please remember always, is the purpose of the thing. Every physical thing has a purpose; consequently it has a SPIRITUAL CORRESPONDENCE. By letting your thoughts dwell upon the purpose of any physical organ, or thing, you make direct and most powerful CONTACT with the SOURCE OF ALL THINGS, with the FIRST CAUSE which projected forth from itself all concentrated things; for as Troward told me, "MATTER IS ONLY SPIRIT SLOWED DOWN TO A POINT OF VISIBILITY."

PUPIL: These examples will help me very much, I am sure. But now I am wondering just what is the best way to help ourselves, and others, forget human weaknesses, aches and pains, etc. It seems to me that most of us have the habit of dwelling too much in thought upon such negative things.

MASTER: I find that the very best way to get away from negative thoughts and feelings is this: TO DELIBERATELY TRAIN THE THOUGHT AND FEELING TO TRAVEL ALONG THE ROAD OF OUR **BLESSINGS!** Our every conscious moment DOES HAVE a blessing in it, if only one will look carefully for it, **recognize** it and **be happy** because of it. In looking for our blessings it will help greatly to recall to mind the many joys we have experienced, as well as those we hope to experience. In these ways we are able to forget the negative things of which the human side of us is so prone to accuse us.

PUPIL: May we have an illustration of this point, please? Something out of your own experience?

MASTER: Yes. Here is an actual experience in which I had a part. In Los Angeles several years ago a lady came to me with the problem of cancer, with which inharmony she had been told that she was grievously afflicted. Her **whole** attention, it seemed to me, was rigidly held on the limitation the cancerous condition was causing her, or should soon cause her to know. She owned and operated a restaurant, and was doing much of the work herself. Several doctors, she said, had told her there was no cure for her, that the disease had spread until an operation was not to be considered, that she must stay off her feet and spend most of her time, such as remained to her, in bed, etc. This, she said, meant that she must go out of business, of course, and when she did that she would be in dire want, in fact an object of charity. With her mind filled with these negative thoughts of illness and lack, which were certain to come unless she could be healed, she came to see me.

When I had talked the matter over with her I asked her to let me think things over for three days before giving her my decision about accepting her case for mental treatment. I asked for this delay in order that I might thoroughly check to see how much time I could allot to her, to see if I could arrange for all the time she would require. After two days of changing some appointments, and postponing some others which were not really urgent, I told the lady to come. My first question to her was this:

"Do you **absolutely BELIEVE** what Jesus told His disciples, as recorded in Mark 10:27, and which reads as follows: 'With man it is impossible, but **not** with God; FOR WITH GOD ALL THINGS ARE POSSIBLE!' ?"

She assured me positively that she DID BELIEVE just that; but said that she found her own mind too untrained and chaotic to keep her thought and feeling OFF what **seemed** to be the inevitable and hold it ON THE FACT that God IS the ONLY POWER there is, that HE is FOREVER PRESENT, ALWAYS AMENABLE TO SUGGESTION, ETERNALLY RESPONSIVE AND ALWAYS CREATIVE. Hence she wished the help of the Spirit through me.

I told her that I should ask her to know with me HOURLY, **continually,** that her relation to God is always I-AM, and that whenever she thought or said "I-AM" to remember that she was thinking or saying, in reality, "GOD IS." I told her also that God created her **out of Himself, for Himself,** and that to **Him and in Him** she was forever **complete, whole, perfect.** "God is love!" I told her; and I asked her to always try to feel His Great Love surging through her. I quoted I John 4:16-18 to her: "God is love; and he that DWELLETH IN LOVE DWELLETH IN GOD and GOD IN HIM!" I also asked her to know that God is LIFE, Intelligent, Loving, Harmonious, Creative Life, and asked her to HOLD HER CONSCIOUS THOUGHT AND FEELING on these things.

"But," she protested, "you have not given me any affirmation for MY cancer!"

"Did you say 'My cancer'?" I asked her with much feeling and emphasis. "Do you really want cancer, my dear? Are you determined to have it? If not, then why ARE YOU CLAIMING IT FOR YOUR OWN by saying 'my cancer'? Remember thoughts are things!"

"Oh, no!" she exclaimed. "I see what you mean. Just listen to me. I must conquer this negative habit of thought."

I assured her yet again that she WAS a Divine Child, that all of her needs were forever supplied THROUGH HER

RECOGNITION of them. I then told her to try to constantly keep in her consciousness thoughts which contained some quality of the following:

Belief	Honesty
Confidence	Patience
Conviction	Reliance
Credit	Sincerity

and other ideas in which there was some of the ESSENCE OF FAITH. I stressed the fact that by keeping these things in mind her THOUGHT and FEELING would have the ESSENCE of FAITH in them; and that she should soon form the HABIT of thinking in that way. It was my endeavor to get her to keep her mind OFF HERSELF and **ON** THE THINGS OF THE SPIRIT. I knew that if I could get her to do this HABITUALLY God should take care of the rest of the matter.

This lady assured me that she would try to do exactly as I had asked although it seemed more plausible to doubt than to believe that she could be in perfect health again after so much suffering, and the opinions of several doctors that she was doomed.

Still again I told her most positively that it is written: "GOD IS WITH YOU TO SAVE YOU!" I asked her to remember that FAITH IS **ALIVE** and that it LEADS TO MORE LIFE which doubt is dead and leads nowhere. The leading characteristic of faith is that it constantly flows and burns with constantly increasing brightness and expectancy. Faith always travels in the one direction of **understanding.** Doubt is a blight upon every effort towards Truth.

This patient came to see me regularly every day for some two weeks; and her condition began to improve from the very start. Then she had only absent treatment at frequent intervals, with an occasional visit in person, for another six weeks. At the end of two months she was

entirely free from any evidences of cancer, free in body, in mind and in affairs. Immediately she began to build up physically and when I last saw her, some two of three years after she first came to me, she was in robust health, prospering in business and sure of her contact with the Spirit.

PUPIL: This illustration clears up in my mind, when I go back over it point by point, a number of ideas which were very hazy and uncertain to me. Thank you. I do know that doubts make one wretched from morning until night.

MASTER: Exactly so. And it would seem that after a while people who indulge in them would learn this fact and make an "about face" and a "forward march" in the direction of faith. Faith is a brightly-glowing light and lives within us. It has its source in the fountain-head of INTUITION. Its radiance is seen in the long shafts of splendor that lead one forever upward into the kingdom of the beautiful, the true, and the good.

PUPIL: If one does not have any faith, how does one get it?

MASTER: One does **NOT** get faith. EVERY SOUL ALREADY HAS IT! It has been yours forever; it is as much a part of you, of your Divine Being, as is your heart, your lungs, your mind: It is a gift as precious as Life itself, and is born of Life itself, forever innate in every living soul. It is true that some are less aware of faith than others through having neglected it, through having blighted it with doubts, fears, anxiety, etc. But the quality IS still there, and by cultivation it will spring into fullness again. All that is required is this: THAT YOU EXERCISE THE FAITH THAT YOU ALREADY HAVE for just a few weeks. Deliberately look for it! Insist on seeing it! **PERSIST IN USING IT!**

LESSON X: IS DESIRE A DIVINE IMPULSE?

MASTER: Is desire a Divine Impulse? One hears this question asked in as many different forms, it seems, as there are humans. So frequently is it propounded and discussed it seems to me that it will be helpful to answer it from Troward's standpoint; after you have studied and meditated upon it from his views you will arrive at your own satisfactory conclusion.

PUPIL: I am glad that you have brought this up for us. I have often wished I knew just what God wanted me to do when I have been undecided about some move, perhaps a momentous decision.

MASTER: The only way anyone can fully understand Life's law of attraction is through seeing what it does under certain given conditions. In a tree it is growth; in an animal it is development; in all of nature it is evolution. From the lowest to the highest forms all growth is prompted by the organized creature pushing forth in its own accomplishment. One can not do otherwise than believe in the law of unfoldment which is the hallowed desire of the All-Originating Life to see ITSELF more and more fully manifested. Since we as humans are branches of the one and only tree of Life this fact is also true of us.

PUPIL: May I ask a question, please?

MASTER: Certainly, any time.

PUPIL: Do you mean that **all** growth is a result of a DESIRE for self-expression, that all evolution is within the great Creative Mind?

MASTER: Just so; and each of us is a direct result of that desire. Therefore we should learn to TRUST OUR DESIRES! There is but the ONE GREAT DESIRE and practically all of our individual desires are reflections of that one. Man's desire, his REAL desire, is for GOOD. No rational person would desire anything else for himself or another.

PUPIL: But many philosophies teach that we must conquer, must overcome, must rise above all desire in order to be perfected. How do you answer this?

MASTER: I stand fast in what has already been said herein. I hold fast to the firm conviction that our desires ARE DIVINE IMPULSES which **stimulate** us to GROWTH and CONSTANT DEVELOPMENT. Without desires we should be mere automatons, should have no wish to progress and grow. It is impossible for one to crush out all desires without RUINING self, spirituality, physically, morally and mentally. The desires, the longings, we have are STIMULI, are URGES for EXPRESSION, from the holy citadel of God within ourselves!

PUPIL: Is it true then that if we would draw into us any particular benefit we have only to impress the desire for it firmly upon the subconscious phase of mind and hold it unwaveringly? Should we do this just as an impression of sound is made upon a phonograph disk before being reproduced? Should we do this knowing that said desire is **instantly transmitted** into the One Great Creative Energy which is always responsive, and that is sure to be manifested in our own physical world?

MASTER: That is just what I mean. Let me give you another illustration. I know a very fine and very wise lady in Los Angles who after returning from marketing found that she had misplaced her car keys; and she had an urgent appointment awaiting her downtown within a little while. She had taken her groceries from the car into the kitchen. After looking around for the keys in every place that she could logically think of she had still failed to find them. So she told herself (her subconscious phase of mind); "I **want** those car keys. I **must** have them. Now where are they? YOU KNOW!" Almost immediately she had the desire to empty the bag of potatoes into the kitchen sink. But she ridiculed that idea, and repeated her desire to find the keys. She did this two or three times, meanwhile keeping up her search for the keys; and every time she received back the feeling that she should empty the potato-bag. It was her habit to let her maid empty the bags and put the purchases away; and the idea of emptying the potato-bag seemed foolish anyway. But the impulse remained urgently with her although she could not see how her car keys could possibly be in the potato-bag. So she did empty the bag into the sink and almost instantly she hear a metallic sound. She looked and, behold, there were the missing keys!

PUPIL: Her deep desire to find the keys brought her the answer? It seems very simple.

MASTER: And it IS very simple once you know the responsiveness of the law of subjective mind. This lady knew that law.

PUPIL: If she really knew the law why did she not recognize the answer to her desires the very first time she was impressed to empty the potato-bag?

MASTER: The lady to whom I refer is a very highly-educated woman, a keen student of logic. While she truly does believe in the intuitive power of the mind to capture an idea from the Infinite the old **race-habit** of giving REASON first place had not been entirely uprooted from her consciousness. When intuition told her plainly to empty the bag reason set up an argument and told her that the impulse was foolish. The controversy between reason and intuition continued within her for several minutes. Then because of her study of Truth, and her application of it, she was reminded that INTUITION, and not logic, IS THE TRUE KEY OF LIFE! So she was impelled to do as she was bidden. When she did so her desire had fulfillment as its correlative. Always DESIRE and FULFILLMENT are bound together as CAUSE and EFFECT through the universal law of attraction!

PUPIL: It still seems to me that a true student of Truth should have thoughts, feelings and desires so trained in the right direction that logic could not go wrong in its conclusions.

MASTER: One does not change life-long habits of reasoning overnight. Like everything else, **complete change** is a matter of growth. The fact that she did obey the still small voice within, and that thus was her problem solved, are all that really mattered. In time this lady, like all of us, will learn to instantly recognize the voice of intuition when it speaks and will no longer question, nor reason, will ONLY OBEY. When we all reach that point, as we can and shall through faithful study and practice, there will be NO PROBLEM IN ALL OF HUMAN EXPERIENCE THAT WILL FAIL TO YIELD ITS ANSWER! There is a lot of truth in old saying:

"Take care of the heart and the head will take care of itself."

PUPIL: But is not the road to the attainment of true wisdom a long, hard one?

MASTER: It is long alright, being Infinite in scope; but it is NOT hard. It is like the story of the two men who are walking to Rome. One asked the other why he had chosen a road that was so full of stones. His companion replied that he had not been aware of any stones in the road, and suggested that they sit down by the roadside and take off their shoes. This they did; and the one who had been complaining found a PEBBLE IN HIS SHOE. But there was nothing wrong with the road itself.

PUPIL: The road is then what each one makes of it for himself? Is that your idea?

MASTER: That is right. The broad highway of Truth is in fact, to me at least, the most interesting road in all of life. It takes times and interesting, **happy** effort to establish an unbroken consciousness of the PERFECT RECIPROCAL ACTION between the **desire for expression** as it exists in the Creative Energy **and** in the individual mind. It is true that by RIGHTLY ESTABLISHING our relation to the Great Parent Mind we can gradually grow into any condition that we may desire, provided of course that we first make of ourselves, through our **habitual** mental attitude, the PERSON WHO CORRESPONDS to those conditions. One can never get away from the Law of Correspondences. This SCIENCE of Correspondence, or of CAUSE and EFFECT, is as infallible as is mathematics; and as in mathematics its principles must be mastered before one can habitual feel: "My Father and I are ONE!" Yes, our DESIRES are our own IMMORTAL SELVES SEEKING FULLER EXPRESSION; and one may soon prove to the doubting, bewildered self that one CAN ABSOLUTELY TRUST THE DESIRES.

PUPIL: Somehow it is still a little difficult for me to accept the feeling that my desires are Divine impulses, or the Divine Nature Itself seeking expression through me. It seems to me that desire is selfish and often wrong, even bad for one.

MASTER: Did not Jesus say: "**Seek** and ye shall find!" Just why would anybody seek a thing?

PUPIL: Because he **wanted** that for which he was seeking.

MASTER: Very good. Are not wants and DESIRES the same? Jesus also said: "ASK believing that you have and ye shall have!" Why would one **ask** for a thing?

PUPIL: Because he desires it and feels it would be good for him.

MASTER: Correct. Yet again the Master said: "Except ye become as a little child ye shall in no wise enter the kingdom of heaven." If one desires to grow into the NEW LIFE OF LIBERTY and JOY, indeed one must become as a little child.

PUPIL: And just what did Jesus mean by that?

MASTER: Just what He said. Observe a child, any child, rich or poor. Its very impulse is desire, is to want something. All children are simply one continual incarnation of "gimme" and "want to." Naturally the child's wants are but the forerunner of the man and his wants; and in the adult desires are as natural as in the child.

PUPIL: This desire idea is truly a new one to me. But I like it.

MASTER: You will learn to love and trust your desires as your spiritual understanding expands. Vitality, which is Life, is born of desire, is the child of Love. You will be amazed at the rapid progress you will make once you have really made up your own mind to **trust your desires.** The more you learn to trust your wants the greater will be your flow of faith.

PUPIL: But must there not be a check somewhere on desires? A sorting of the good and the bad? All desires are not holy, are they?

MASTER: One must be rational, of course. Troward writes in his "Edinburgh Lectures" that "there is nothing wrong with the evidences of a HEALTHY MIND in a HEALTHY BODY." This study presupposes that a sincere student of Truth will not harbor evil desires, that his or her mentality is normal, the behavior normal. This being so the desires of such a one should also be only natural, rational, good; and if this is so then the desires of that one are Divine impulses. Let me suggest that you read the personal letter that Troward wrote to me, an exact copy of which is found in my book, "Attaining Your Desires," on pages 135 and 136. Then you will see yet more clearly why you should TRUST YOUR DESIRES, recognizing as you do that DESIRES ARE DIVINE IMPULSES!

LESSON XI: SUPREME SELF-FREEDOM

PUPIL: So, SUPREME SELF-FREEDOM is our very wonderful subject for today, is it? I am sure that you shall prove to us that supreme self-freedom can be ours, that MIND DOES RULE THE WORLD.

MASTER: You may always be quite certain that **YOUR MIND RULES YOUR WORLD;** and you may always know that your individual world is a branch of the Universal World. Your mind makes of your world a thing of BEAUTY, PEACE and ABSOLUTE FREEDOM, **if only you so will.**

PUPIL: I am convinced that this is true IF only one could truly **control one's** mind, thoughts and feelings at all times. I know that others have attained this mastery, this self control; but somehow it does not seem to be for me, as much as I desire it.

MASTER: At one time in our lives each of us thought this same thing about the multiplication-tables. How difficult they seemed to us as children; yet each of us mastered them by PERSISTENT EFFORT. It is like that with ABSOLUTE SELF-FREEDOM. It is dormant within each soul, waiting only for us to **call** upon it, to **arouse** it, to **recognize** it, to give it our attention, our concentrated observation, in our every **thought,** our every feeling, every act. It is **not** difficult to have if we make it **FIRST** in our lives just as a great scientist puts his science BEFORE EVERYTHING ELSE! In theory at least all of us realize that we get only what we REACH FOR and REACH FOR STEADILY.

PUPIL: Is not Annette Kellerman, the great swimmer, an example of this? Was she not a cripple as a child, and considered hopelessly crippled?

MASTER: Yes, she was. But through insistent, persistent, determined, steady effort she became the physically-perfect woman, a model for the women of the world. Her science was the science of health, the science of physical beauty and perfection. There are many sciences; and each of us may select the one with which we are most in tune and pursue it to a dazzling goal.

PUPIL: But has not science boasted that it has DIS-proved the Holy Bible?

MASTER: It may be that some scientists make this boast. But it is **not** true. The fact of the matter is that SCIENCE HAS CONFIRMED THE TRUTH OF THE BIBLE! It might be said that science has written a **new** Bible for the THINKING mind merely by clarifying the old one. Science has made of the Bible the Book supreme for those who are determined to live **HERE** and **NOW**. Science has proved that "THE WORD" of Life, of the Spirit, IS A LIVING WORD OF POWER! Truly "the heavens do declare the glory of God, and the firmament sheweth His handiwork."

In reading your Bible always substitute the word "Subconscious Mind" for the word "Lord." Try this faithfully for awhile and see what an **astonishing** growth you will make. Try this with such passages as Isaiah 40:31, Mark 29:30, Luke 18:29-30 and a host of others. Look about you; look at the results achieved by those who have learned to

LOVE, to USE and to TRUST the MIND. Strength, power, beauty, television, wire-photography, microscope, telescope, spectroscope, all of these, yes ALL of ALL THINGS, are **RESULTS** from the Great Creative Energy whose progress, harmony; telephone, wireless, airplanes, chief attributes are these:

1. It is EVER-PRESENT, EVERYWHERE;

2. It is always AMENABLE to suggestion;

3. It is FOREVER RESPONSIVE;

4. It is ETERNALLY **CREATIVE.**

This God-ENERGY, **REMEMBER,** manifests in the MIND OF MAN, in fact IS the mind of man. The three Bible-references given above, and many others, teach us that if one puts the DEVELOPMENT of the DIVINE SPARK WITHIN **FIRST,** over **all else,** the DIVINE in return will make that one **FIRST** with it! Truly then the BEST Life has to give is the possession of that one!

PUPIL: Am I right in believing that the precious promises of the Bible all hinge upon our making intelligent, Loving Life (God) FIRST in everything? And if I do is EVERYTHING I may desire sure to be mine?

MASTER: That is right, IF YOU MAKE GOD **FIRST,** if you **really** DO make Him FIRST. That is to say we should make it our FIRST effort to KNOW LIFE'S LAWS and TO LIVE THEM! In this connection please read over and over again, or better still MEMORIZE letter perfect, the 22nd Chapter of Job, beginning at verse 21 and continuing to the end of the Chapter. The promises given there, the power, the freedom, the plenty, ARE yours, exactly as promised, if you will take the time, the effort, to become ACQUAINTED with the LOVING PARENT-POWER which is always ABLE, and ever MORE THAN WILLING to do these things IN YOU, THROUGH YOU. As you read be **sure** to bear in mind constantly that the 21st verse is the KEY to all of the others that follow it. The gist of this whole passage in Job is this: **WE GET OUT OF LIFE EXACTLY WHAT WE PUT INTO IT, PLUS MUCH INCREASE AS INTEREST ON OUR FAITH!** Some state this in a more homely way by saying that "we get what we pay for, and no more."

PUPIL: I have often wondered about this in connection with tithing. Is it true that tithing is a very old Law which has the greatest power back of it?

MASTER: Indeed tithing IS A LAW which has MUCH POWER in it! I have tithed for twenty-five years, religiously so. The practice of tithing is a divine-habit-forming virtue. People tithe because they recognize God and wish to DEVELOP their recognition and expectancy. Regular, systematic tithers are those who have formed the HABIT of **COUNTING THEIR BLESSINGS.** As a result their BLESSINGS CONSTANTLY INCREASE! Did not Abraham give a tenth of his ALL to Melchizedek as a TOKEN of acknowledgment that his SUCCESSES WERE FROM GOD? And when Jesus sent His disciples forth into the cities of Israel He expressly forbade them to take with them any money or provisions. Why? Because He wished the people of those cities to **recognize God in His servants,** and to support them with their tithes. As Saint Paul said: "The people who receive spiritual instruction shall administer some of their GOOD to him who gives the instruction." IT IS a FACT abundantly PROVED that the **HABIT** OF TITHING IS A **SURE ROAD** TO **SUPREME SELF-FREEDOM!**

PUPIL: Am I to understand that the habit of tithing would give me a consciousness of an ABIDING PARTNERSHIP WITH GOD? Because my tithing is to God and His servants? Is this correct? Does one tithe to God's cause in recognition, in loving recognition, of Divine guidance? Does one necessarily have to tithe to churches only?

MASTER: No, one need not tithe to churches only. Some people tithe regularly to missionary organizations, some to charities, and many tithe to individuals who work in God's vineyards, irrespective of organizations or affiliations. The value of tithing lies in the ESTABLISHMENT OF THE FEELING OF CONSTANT DIVINE PARTNERSHIP. Tithing brings one into the HIGH and FRUITFUL CONSCIOUSNESS of GOD AND COMPANY, **UN**limited! If one keeps in CONSCIOUS touch with the Ever-Present, Responsive Substance of Life by regularly returning to it some of the substance (funds) which it has placed in his stewardship, this constitutes a practical acknowledgment of blessings and thus INCREASES THE BLESSINGS MANYFOLD. The ancient Israelites PROVED this fact consistently; and for centuries the Jews have practiced tithing, as they do to-day. The Mormons of to-day prove this Law constantly also. When I was lecturing in Salt Lake City during the "Depression" there was not a SINGLE MORMON, or MORMON FAMILY ON RELIEF! The reason is obvious. THEY TITHE!

PUPIL: I did not realize that tithing was so very great a stimulant for the steady inflow of supply; but now it seems to me that it would give one the same sense of security one has when the taxes are paid in full.

MASTER: That is right. After all your money is yourself; You are God's, your money is His also. Humanity exchanges its abilities, integrity, labor, etc., for money. In my thirty-five years as a practitioner I have had thousands of people come to me for spiritual help for increased supply; BUT in all of that time I have NEVER HAD A SOLITARY TITHER seek my help for financial increase! In fact I have had very few tithers, ones who religiously follow the practice, ever seek my help for ANY KIND OF INHARMONY! Tithing DOES carry with it a WEALTH OF BLESSINGS. **GIVING IS WORSHIP!** If one REALLY worships God, and considers Him one's BEST business partner, one acknowledges His help by giving to His cause **FIRST.** The average person gives a mere pittance to God, AFTER they have paid everything else. That is NOT tithing in any sense. A tithe is not a tithe unless it is ten per cent. The tithe should be paid **first,** from the **gross** profit; and it should be tendered in genuine love, thanksgiving and joy, if not in sheer abandon.

PUPIL: Is tithing required by the Intelligent, Creative Power in Life? Surely God does not need the money, or lands, or cattle.

MASTER: Tithing is voluntary. Yet it IS REQUIRED if one wishes a **continual increase** of blessings. It is a great joy to recognize God as a partner. To me a partner means one of whom we are fond, with whom we labor for a common good, and with whom we happily SHARE in love. In order to receive benefits from tithing there MUST be JOY IN GIVING. To tithe grudgingly yields no blessings, or few at best. "He who gives HIMSELF with his gifts feeds three, himself, his hungering neighbor and ME!" Tithing brings with it an ABIDING SENSE OF SECURITY, has within its loving bosom an abundance of SUCCESS-IDEAS which when adopted bring health, wealth and happiness. This is the LAW OF TITHING.

PUPIL: Thank you for this lesson on tithing. I should like to hear much more about it. But are you going to tell us to-day how to reason ourselves into certainty?

MASTER: This is hardly what I meant when we were discussing reasoning out an affirmation before trying to absorb it. For example let us consider freedom. Freedom is joy; joy is freedom. But it seems there are few who have either freedom or joy to any great extent. Many seem to be bound by miseries; their every day is full of discord. To them work, all kinds of work, is disagreeable. To them most people are unbearable; things that happen are awful. The weather is abominable; it rains when it shouldn't; when it should rain it doesn't. They buy things, then regret it. They sell things and then are hurt because they didn't receive more money. If they don't go places they feel slighted; if they do go places they feel sure they were snubbed. If they don't have things they are despondent; if they do have things they are not what they want, etc., etc., etc.

PUPIL: Heavens, is this the average person you are describing?

MASTER: No. I am just giving you an intimate glimpse of a person in bondage, of ones who have not trained their minds to HOLD ONLY THOUGHTS OF ABSOLUTE FREEDOM. Perfect joy and freedom and yours NOW. TAKE them and make them YOURS.

PUPIL: How may one enter upon these joy thoughts at will?

MASTER: That is the place for the affirmation. Take, for example, the thought: "THE VERY BEST LIFE HAS TO GIVE IS MINE NOW!" Reason about this for a minute. Why is it true? Because Life (God) made me out of Himself and LIVES IN ME. The very life of me is God. Life is happy; life is free; life is health; life is wealth; Life is ALL GOOD.

PUPIL: I can see this **BUT** suppose that when you have satisfied yourself this is true some member of the family, or some friend, jabs you with a very unkind remark? What then? Are you supposed to laugh that off?

MASTER: If you REALLY ARE CONSCIOUS that the BEST Life has to give is yours, you will instantly realize at all times that you are not supposed to try to live **for** another. You have all you can do to keep the stream of joy flowing through your own consciousness. When I first began my study with Troward he cautioned me every day: **"Watch your THOUGHTS and FEELINGS! They DO TAKE FORM, you know!"** And he really got that great Truth across to my consciousness. When I went to Ruan Manor to study with him, I had been accustomed to a personal maid all of my life. I took my maid with me when I went to Troward. There was not one modern convenience where I lived Ruan Manor; and none could be obtained thereabouts. We had been there just a month when Marie came to me in tears and told me she was heartbroken to leave me but she could not stay in that awful place any longer; she just must go back to Paris. She was too lonely, etc. Of course my first thoughts were: "If Marie goes, what shall I do? Here we are miles from anywhere, with no conveniences of any kind. What does this mean? Why should this disaster come to me now, of all times, when I really am trying to know God?" Just when my thoughts reached that station, and were gathering momentum, Troward's warning: **"WATCH YOUR THOUGHTS!"** came to my mind and I stopped right there. I began to use the will exercise he had taught me. I also used affirmations he had given me, to hold my thoughts where the Creative Power in THOUGHTS AND FEELINGS could produce **what I wanted.** What I wanted most was FREEDOM TO CONTINUE WITH MY STUDY. I deliberately held my thoughts in the RIGHT place. Only two days later the lady from whom I rented our rooms came to me and said she believed that Marie had been trying to tell her that she was leaving me (Marie was French and spoke no English) and that she wished she could find me another good personal maid before she went to Paris. I told the lady this was the case. She said that her daughter was coming home from London in just a few days, that her daughter had worked there for several years as a good personal maid, and that she felt sure the girl would be happy to work for me in that capacity. Marie left after teaching the other girl just how I wished things done; and the new maid was as satisfactory as the first. In this episode I had my first good lesson in knowing that I must WATCH MY THOUGHTS, that THEY DO BECOME THINGS!

PUPIL: You have said that your favorite affirmation is the Lord's Prayer. Please show us how you would reason this out in order to better understand it before using it, part of it at least.

MASTER: Very well. The first two words of that prayer carry a tremendous power, if they are thought over, or spoken, with much feeling. What does "Our Father" suggest? Our Father, our very own Father? When you were a child what was your idea of your father? Your idea of him may have been exaggerated but you BELIEVED him to be rich beyond all words, influential, kind, loving, good, always ready to give, to help, to comfort, to make you happy and to see that you had everything that your little heart could desire. Then try to feel yourself as a child of **God**, with all the enthusiasm of a child. Know that you are so like HIM that He adores you, guides you, shields you, protects you, gives you everything He has to give in generous quantity, that you are, and that you have, HIS ALL. Do this with the whole prayer. Think about it all, understand and assimilate it all; then USE IT ALL! If you will do your part you will find that the Father-Principle in life IS ALWAYS RESPONSIVE! Your objective quality of mind may not know what is best for you because it can only realize the objective and limited side of Life. But THE FATHER IN YOU, HE KNOWS! Ask Him, be guided by Him. Your real desires are but reflections from Him which shine through and register in your mind.

PUPIL: Would it not be a good idea for us to frequently refer back to the lesson on "Desire, a Divine Impulse" when there is any confusion of mind about desires?

MASTER: Yes, that is recommended; in fact I trust that you will frequently review **all** of the Lessons of this Course. And I devoutly wish that you would earnestly TRY to MAKE GOD **FIRST** in your heart, and mind, and soul, and daily and hourly life. **If** you will, it will mean for you a life of SUPREME SELF-FREEDOM and truly you will MAKE OF YOURSELF a reflection of God's OWN IDEA who is the PERFECTED you. To this end I recommend the following, all of which I urge you to **memorize,** letter perfect. I also URGE you to USE and USE and yet again USE these points and affirmations, faithfully and regularly. Here they are:

For DAILY, Systematic, Loving **Use:**

Your **hourly** effort should be that of fully realizing your **true** place in the Great Plan of Life.

Just what is this TRUE place for each individual? It is, as Troward taught me, the following three things:

1. WORSHIP of God **Alone;**

2. The absolute EQUALITY of all individuals;

3. **Complete** CONTROL of all else.

Affirmations:

1. I AM intelligent, Loving Spirit, LIVING in Creative Love and Power! In Him do I LIVE and MOVE and have my WHOLE BEING!

2. I AM a specialized PART OF God's own Self-Manifestation! God IS **specialized** in **me;** therefore I AM perfect Harmony!

3. I AM direct knowledge of ALL Truth! I AM perfect Intuition! I AM Spiritual perception at its fullness! There is but ONE Wisdom; therefore I AM Perfect Wisdom!

4. My mind IS a center of DIVINE operation; therefore I AM always thinking good thoughts, speaking **only con**structive words! Time is Eternal; God is the ONLY Giver! His Loving Intelligence is **continually** working IN and THROUGH me; hence I AM ever working correctly. I AM thinking the RIGHT thoughts, in the RIGHT way, at the RIGHT time, towards the RIGHT result! God's work IN and THROUGH **me** is always WELL done!

5. I AM Specialized Spirit! I AM always receiving rich, powerful inspirations from the Great, Universal, Parent Spirit. Divine Intelligence is always thinking NEW, FRESH, CLEAR ideas through me, ones far beyond any I have ever known before. My prayers are the outflow of the Great Oversoul of the Universe. They go forth in His Name; and ALWAYS they ACCOMPLISH that for which I send them. GOD **IS** GLORIFYING HIMSELF **IN** AND **THROUGH** ME NOW!

LESSON XII: LIVE LIFE AND LOVE IT!

1. Breathing, Bathing and Short, Easy, Profitable Exercises for Health:

Note: (These exercises are given as a stimulant to your capacity, both mental and physical. Mind and body are **one.** When both body and mind are strong happiness and success usually follow, especially if one adds to them mental and bodily efficiency.)

Correct breathing is one of Nature's most powerful methods of building a powerful body, a perfect body. Let us begin now to breathe correctly and **profitably.** If these exercises are taken as intended there will not be any strain. The first exercise is this:

Upon arising in the morning first drink two or three glasses of water. The effect will be better if you will take the water just as hot as you can bear to drink it, with the juice of one-half a lemon in it. Then stand erect, or else lie flat on the floor. Exhale **completely.** Whether standing or lying on floor bend knees slightly. As you exhale contract **both** the chest and the **diaphragm,** pushing the latter OUT and DOWN as far as possible without causing strain. Naturally this will extend the abdomen. Then **without lifting your chest** pull abdomen IN as far as you can. Then without any attempt at correct breathing push abdomen OUT and IN rapidly at least twelve times.

After you have mastered the above exercise for the abdomen and diaphragm, take the next exercise--for not more than two minutes each time. This exercise is: Stand erect, or lie flat on the back. Exhale completely, contracting chest. Then slowly inhale through the nostrils, trying not to allow chest to move. Let the diaphragm push the abdomen down, then hold the breath for three or four seconds. Exhale slowly. Then forget all about abdomen and diaphragm and inhale deeply, letting breath lift chest walls up and out to their fullest capacity. Hold breath a few seconds and exhale all the breath.

If you will practice these two simple exercises each morning for ten days, you will note a great improvement in physical condition and vitality, the head and mind will be clearer and you will have a real zest for work.

No doubt you know that the right kind of bath is a splendid nerve-tonic, as well as a most important point in attaining physical and mental perfection. When bathing for cleanliness the water should be of blood temperature, never hot or cold. **After** the cleansing bath, fill the wash-basin with cold water. Scoop up two handfuls and apply to the forehead, and rub up and down the face. Dip hands in cold water again and shake off all surplus water, then rub off balance behind the ears. Repeat process on back of neck. These things soothe and strengthen the nerves.

2. A certain way of relief for constipation is this: First, meditate on the perfect and harmonious action of Life. In Nature one does not find either inaction or over-action. Think over how the Life in your body regulates the flow of blood, the action of the muscles, both voluntary and involuntary, and how all of these things are done in perfect harmony. For a regulatory exercise in relieving constipation the following is splendid. **First,** as soon as you arise in the morning, drink two glasses of **hot** water. Then stand, or lie

on the back on floor. Breathe deeply. As you inhale extend the abdomen and contract it as you exhale, contracting it all you possibly can. Do this without letting chest rise at all. Do the exercise rapidly, vigorously, always inhaling through the nostrils and exhaling through the mouth. Take about eight seconds for each complete breath. Do this for a minute or two then use another minute to recover normal breathing. A second exercise is recommended; and it is better if taken in connection with the one just given. It is this: Again stand erect or lie on the back, preferably the latter. Draw first the right knee and then the left up to the chest as snug as possible. Inhale deeply as you put foot down to floor and exhale as you draw knee down to chest. Do this exercise rapidly, vigorously for one minute. After the exercise try to get into the **feeling** of gratitude that you ARE able to CONSCIOUSLY tune in with the harmonious action of Life. If you keep thinking deeply on the fact that ALL of the qualities of Life must be present anywhere and everywhere that Life is, the feeling of ONE-ness will come and you will enjoy the thrill of it. The very best there is is yours **now** and the perfect movement **is** manifesting NOW.

3. How to Retain Youth and to Banish Gray Hairs and Wrinkles if They Offend You:

Think, know, feel, be thankful for the fact that Life as Life has NO age and yet is ageless. Give this fact a little profound thought every day. Soon you will get the deep and abiding **awareness** of it. In your mind's eye, and in memory, try to recall how you felt about certain things when you were twenty, how you looked then, and acted, and bubbled over with energy. Ask yourself if your point of view about Life in general has changed radically, or if you have simply forgotten how to Live Life and Love it, as you did then. The emotions, the fine understanding, the zest for activity, as you had them in youth have not glided off without leaving a trace in the development of your advancing years. Try to give yourself a careful going over mentally each day, and

LIVE for a while each day the experiences of your youth, bringing them back into your FEELING. Perhaps you say: "Oh, but youth is so foolish!" That may be so; but remember always that it DOES THINGS! Try to weed out and destroy the doubts of your advancing years; try to prune out of yourself, out of your thought and feeling, your tendency towards being over-conservative. Old age is only an OSSIFIED IDEA! Being over-conservative and opposed to progress and change are the things that make one old, and usually impotent. Your youth was all right; LIVE IT AGAIN! Live it in FEELING and keep the feeling bolstered temporarily by making mental pictures of your happy, cocksure self as you were at twenty. SEE your face, figure and hair as they were then. And **each day** do the following exercise for the banishment of gray hair. Vigorously RUB the whole scalp, from the nape of the neck up over the crown to the hair-line on the forehead, using Glover's Mange Cure. This liquid is not for dogs only, but is also an excellent tonic and stimulant for human hair. Rub the liquid well into the scalp. The gray hair may fall out for a while after you have done this exercise faithfully for several days but keep it up and new hair will come in with the natural color of the hair of your youth. Yes, mentally go back to twenty and balance its vitality with your present wisdom! KNOW with all of your heart and soul, and all of your emotional self, that Life as Life IS manifesting in you in a particular way in order that it may find new avenues for expressing itself as the JOY of living. Make an **hourly** effort to keep in your consciousness your JOYS only. MAKE THEM REGISTER! Deliberately BE HAPPY and your body will respond to it in every way. It will also help, particularly for the ladies, to sit in front of the vanity a half-hour each day, seeing yourself NOT as you are now (if aged) but AS YOU WERE in youth. Do this with deep concentration, deepest feeling, affirming something like this: "I AM Life. I AM YOUTH, **eternal** YOUTH!" The important thing, however, is to SEE yourself as youth, to FEEL youth, to know that you ARE youth. Soon you will find a decided improvement setting in. Thought IS **always** creative!

Soon you will look younger; soon you will feel younger; soon you will be younger, not in years of course but years do not make aging. Some are old at twenty-five; others are young at eighty. It is **flexibility** of mind, a keen enjoyment of living, that make for elasticity of muscle and for youth.

4. A Method of Attracting Money:

Meditate on the RICHES of Life as it **really** is. All that we can see or think of in Nature shows us only ABUNDANCE. Every growing thing is **amply** provided for. The grass and tress, and other growing things, do not know poverty. In the soil, in the air, in the sunshine, there is an abundance of nourishment for all. THINK about this great fundamental Truth because it applies to YOU also. Wherever you may be, whatever your station in life may be, the Creator of all Life HAS just as amply provided for you as He has for the grass, the birds, all of Nature. It is not His fault that all do not express or manifest this bounty; people are as poor, or will soon be as rich, as they ACCEPT for themselves in the CONSCIOUSNESS. Everything that your individual nature may require has ALREADY BEEN PROVIDED for you by the Creator. One has only to ACCEPT it, first in consciousness then in fact. Your STEADY RECOGNITION of this fact forms a veritable magnet in the mind which will attract every requirement to you, not as money that will drop in your lap without effort but as **ideas,** which when ACTED UPON, will yield an abundant harvest. Try this. Begin right now to **take the time,** two or three times daily, to focus your thought at the base of the brain: "Spirit of God (Life), I AM GRATEFUL to you for the ABUNDANCE that IS mine **now!**" Any other good affirmation that may appeal to you, one that you compose for yourself perhaps, will do provided the use of it LIFTS your **thought** and **feeling** into CERTAINTY that abundance IS yours **now.** The more completely you can flood your mind, your CONSCIOUSNESS, with the **recognition** of Life's abundance, for you as well as for all, the more quickly your thought and feeling will manifest in FORM. **Rich**

ideas will come to you intuitively, particularly if you impress the RICHES that ARE yours NOW upon your mind just before going to sleep. Any **good** idea if acted upon with wisdom and energy will yield great abundance for any one who apprehends it and works in FAITH towards its fulfillment.

5. The Value of Sleep and a New Method of Inducing It:

Sleep is Nature's restorative for tired tissues and often is found to be the only effective refreshener of the body machine. The exact amount of sleep required varies with different individuals, much depending upon how fatigued a person is when retiring. If one feels the need of relaxation and sleep, and yet can not easily go to sleep, try the following method, which you may have read in my book, "The Healing Power is Life." It is this: Sit nude on the edge of your bathtub, feet **outside** the tub. Take a fountain syringe and fill it with water that is blood-warm (NOT hot). Place the end of the tube at nape of neck and let the warm water trickle down your spine until you begin to feel relaxed; then go to bed quickly, comfortable, warm and relaxed. Another aid towards relaxation (and relaxation, if complete, is sure to induce sleep in a weary person) is this: Lying in bed, on the back, deliberately send the message down to your toes, firmly, **"Relax!"** Continue sending the message until the toes do spread and relax. Then relax ankles in same manner, also knees, then base of spine, and the spine itself to base of head, also hands and arms. As a rule one will never get this far with the relaxation-exercise; almost invariably one will slip off into deep, restful sleep before having **consciously** relaxed more than half the body. Upon awakening if you feel recuperated, don't force yourself to remain in bed, whatever the hour. Get up and do something that you are interested in doing. Be sure the room you sleep in is always well ventilated; almost all people breathe more deeply when sleeping than when awake, unless exercising quite freely. Do not eat a big meal just before retiring.

If you will give this method of inducing sleep a fair trial, you will find it very effective in inducing refreshing sleep that will have a real recuperative value.

LESSON XIII: SUPPLEMENT
"HOW TO LIVE LIFE AND LOVE IT!"

MASTER: If you are anxious and uncertain about the future because of the fast-moving and extremely chaotic changes now going on all about you, here is a lesson that will help you find your true self and to stay at peace. Once we really find the true self we are in tune with Life **as it is.** Then we can live life and love it! Life really is glorious once one knows how to live it. Try to imagine for a few minutes that you know a secret which opens all of the closed doors of seeming limitation and that you can then step into a new world in which all is Life and Liberty. In order to enter this fair paradise of freedom the mind must be trained to choose carefully the emotional trend of thinking.

PUPIL: Do you mean that **only** those who have developed their different mental faculties through study and practice of Truth can enter this kingdom?

MASTER: That is exactly what I mean, since thoughts alone are creative. Those who have leaned the value of the trained will, imagination, intuition, and who live accordingly, can really feel secure. The tendency of thought, the **habits of thought,** determine with precision one's outward affairs. So as you start to travel this road which leads to absolute liberty in all things it is necessary to leave behind all excess baggage such as self pity, intolerance, criticism, fear, despondency, feelings of superiority, and all other negative and destructive occupants of your mental house. Take all these and put them in a secure bag; then tie a string of resolute determination tightly around them and dump them on a trash-pile. Cover the worthless bag of destructive evils with oil and set it on fire. Then are you really ready to start on your journey.

PUPIL: It would seem that one is only able to "go places" on this road by developing self-control. Is that so necessary?

MASTER: Yes, vitally necessary. However true and powerful a truth may be there must be a method of application of the principle to the individual. The best and surest method of manifesting the truth that God and man are **one,** and that **God lives in** and **thinks through** each of us, is to deliberately cultivate self-control with its consequent serenity of mind. In your endeavor to use this great Power for your individual purpose in the affairs of your hourly life you must be able to catch your thought the minute it begins to wander into doubts, fears, condemnations, criticisms, etc. and turn it in the direction you DO wish to go. Thus will you build **certainty** into your soul and body and the possession of certainty **within** means certainty and all things good **in the affairs.**

PUPIL: You make it seem that my disposition and self-control need much of my attention. I will admit that I am not patient; and of course I am intolerant, but only with those who deserve it--only with those who do not seem to try to do their part do I lose my temper.

MASTER: It is not my intention to be personal about your disposition. But I do say earnestly that every person who wishes to enjoy the blessings of true freedom MUST learn careful thought-selection, which means absolute thought-control, or self-control. In this way you will very soon entertain only the thought-guests you admire and enjoy. The uncouth, the grouchy, the selfish, the condemnatory, the suspicious, the **tramp** thoughts, all of whom will try to make a convenience of your mental domain, must be turned out of your mind. The best way to do this is put your whole feeling into an affirmation, whatever one appeals to you at the moment. Hold steadily to that thought and feeling until everything unlike it is out of your mind. Then lock your mental doors and use your will to keep out thoughts you have dismissed from your presence.

PUPIL: This making my mind do my new will is not going to be easy. I will practically have to make over completely my habitual mental processes.

MASTER: No, it will not be easy. But the goal the discipline will lead you to is worth a thousand times the effort required, however much effort that may be. If you will mentally stick tight to your resolve to make your mind a conscious center of divine operation, even for one week, seeing yourself growing steadily into what you wish to become, you will be amazed at your own growth and the genuine interest you have in everything around you. Also you will discover many, many wonderful things about yourself that you never knew before. Now is this all: Once you focus your **at**tention and your intention on the Intelligent Life within you, and try to reproduce it in your own self, you will begin to get results that will seem almost phenomenal to you, and at once. Keep your consciousness focused on the fact that the Spirit of Life has no fears, no anxiety, and soon your feeling will correspond with It. Just try this, say for two weeks, without slipping; then ask yourself if you would go back to your old estate, if you could.

PUPIL: Is one apt to be "hypnotized," and thus hindered in progress, by the thoughts of others about one? Sometimes I seem to be making real progress when suddenly, and for no apparent reason, there is an almost uncontrollable impulse and feeling of **oh what is the use!** I am like a ship without a rudder, trying to plow through some invisible, and invincible, force, and "getting nowhere fast," as the saying is. At best these experiences are long, long detours off the main road. What causes these episodes?

MASTER: You gave it its right name in the beginning. It **is** hypnotism; but as a rule it is self-hypnotism, almost unconsciously done because of the **old habits of thought;** and it comes as the result of your **letting things other than your aim hold your attention.** Your efforts to control your thoughts should be **steady, continuous, with no unguarded moments.** Mere spasmodic efforts, however strongly indulged in at the times of their occurrence to you, will never take you very far on the road to the new goal you have set. Before you study any further in these lessons, **yes right now, make up your mind positively** that you are entering upon the study **to win,** and that you will make an earnest, steady, continuous effort to do so. **My own personal remedy for overcoming any tendency to slip back** into the old rut of wrong thinking, and I assure you that **I have always found it a most potent and sure panacea,** is, believe it or not, that wonderful thing, derisively called "old-fashioned and out of date" by some, -- The Lord's Prayer. Go carefully over the Lord's Prayer every day. If you do not already know it thoroughly, memorize it, so that you can repeat it anywhere, anytime, silently if you like. Us it, repeat it carefully, slowly, and with **much** depth of feeling, as often as there is the least tendency to slip off your path. After you have finished with your reading, or repetition of the Prayer, then take up your mental picture again, mentally **seeing, feeling, believing, knowing that you are already in possession of whatever it is that you want.** This is what Jesus meant when He said for us to always, "ask **believing that ye already have and ye SHALL**

HAVE!" **If** you will do these things, very soon you will find that you ARE on the road to Freedom and Joy, and it will constantly grow easier for you to stay on the highway, without so many detours.

PUPIL: Just now I should like very much to have more money. In fact I must have it. Do you mean that I can attract the money I need by living with the Lord's Prayer for, say half an hour every morning and every night, just "precipitate" the money right out of the very air? That seems incredible!

MASTER: What you ask **is incredible!** And you are not getting my real meaning. The **finest statement** of the **Law** of **Life** ever uttered is, in my opinion, that wonderful, wonderful statement of Jesus, namely: "Seek ye FIRST the kingdom of God and His righteousness (right-use-ness) and (then) **all things** will be added unto you." But please note that FIRST you must seek the kingdom, must make an honest effort to make your mind a center of divine operation **only,** and **for its own sake** and not from any ulterior motive. **Then** will all **things** be added unto you. What happens to you through the steady, persistent use of the Lord's Prayer, as we were discussing it, is this: With the constant change in your mental attitude as you progress you are developing more and more strength and spiritual power. This self-mastery you are steadily developing is the growth of Divine Wisdom, Power and Beauty within you. Naturally then your whole outside world will gradually change to correspond to your new inside world because your most habitual thought takes outward form. Delightful changes will come into the circle of your individual world. Your thought and feeling will attract corresponding shapes; and you will feel much encouraged to go on and on and on into more and more joy and freedom.

SECOND SUPPLEMENT
"HOW TO LIVE LIFE AND LOVE IT!"
IMAGINATION AND INTUITION

MASTER: To-day we shall discuss that great power we call imagination.

PUPIL: May I ask just what imagination is. I have heard you often speak of it as our "spiritual aeroplane," and say that "it wings us." But just what is it?

MASTER: No mortal can possibly answer that question. With all of our scientific research no one has found any rational clue as to the source of this great power, **outside of God or Spirit.** Nor has any one been able to determine how far the use of imagination is able to carry one. It is Infinite. It is the mystery of mysteries; and it might be compared to electricity in this respect. Yet we know it does exist and that its power for good is inconceivable, if **used** constructively, correctly. What we should do is to inquire into its **usefulness** to us. Every normal person is equipped with it to some degree; and like the will the imagination **can be developed.** If rightly understood and correctly used it will perform seeming miracles.

PUPIL: But why do you call imagination the "spiritual aeroplane?"

MASTER: Because imagination, correctly **used,** can and will lift one, as if on wings, above and beyond all limitation, above one's low, narrow views of life, into a cloudless domain of true perspective. Imagination gives one clear vision of possibilities in your life which you have never been able to see before. Then while you realize that it takes **determination** and **effort** to achieve success; you also know that you can, with the imagination, tap the source of unlimited possibilities and Intelligent Energy. In a flash that mysterious, winged thing called imagination shows you where all the riches of Life are to be found.

PUPIL: Suppose one feels weak, obscure, poor, that you know your ideas are good but that you lack the money or health to carry them into effect. What can imagination do about these things?

MASTER: Imagination will reveal that strength and power and means are to be found within your Divine self and that a better and better acquaintance with, and a more frequent use of, the God-powers within is certain to lead to success on any line.

PUPIL: Can imagination lift one to great spiritual heights? Or does it pertain more to material success?

MASTER: Jesus, the Nazarene, lifted himself to the exalted Christhood through understanding and using his powers of imagination. Is that not reaching the heights spiritually?

PUPIL: Is it the imagination that opens the door for limitless good to enter?

MASTER: No, not correctly speaking. It is **intuition,** a feminine, or soul, quality which first captures an idea from the Infinite and passes it on to the imagination. Imagination raises one to a place in consciousness where all things are not only possible but are **present,** spiritual **facts.** Look all about at the ones who have risen above every conceivable handicap to very great success. Let us take Louis Pasteur, for example. He did not have any better mentality, or more strength, or more money, than any other ordinary Frenchman; and he was just as obscure as the lowest of them. His mental tools, by nature, were no sharper than yours are. But that strange and mysterious thing called imagination was very active in him and soared far beyond his scant equipment and early hardships into new realms of wisdom. Many times he was not sure; but he imagined; and because he imagined he **discovered;** and because he discovered he wrought miraculous cures and to this day his wisdom prevents disease and death in countless millions. Truly Pasteur was a saint. The same is true of Paracelsus. People said he was lucky. Envious and lazy people always say this of anyone that succeeds. But the cures of Paracelsus were not luck; they were the result of his imagination and industry. Jesus intimately acquainted himself with God through the use of his fertile imagination; and through use of the same mystic power he was able to enter into other lives. His success easily can be attributed to his ability to see God (which is Perfection) in every person he contacted, however tragic, lonely, hopeless or vicious that one seemed. Through his **recognition** of God in all men he helped men to see God in themselves. **This** was the source of his great power!

PUPIL: Then imagination is a veritable dynamo and not just a means of trivial, idle day-dreaming?

MASTER: Yes. **Recognize** your imagination as a dynamo of limitless power. Use all of it that you possess whenever you need it. **Understanding of it,** and **experience in using**

it, will readily prove it to be the most powerful force in your mental equipment. Used correctly it will carry your light up among the brightest stars of highest heaven. It is not enough to dream and **idly** desire, not any more than it is enough to start an aeroplane's motor just to watch the propeller go round and round. You must fuel your imagination with knowledge and purpose. You must take your bearings and hold your course. Risks, hardships, will be only still greater opportunities to use your imagination in your journey through the clouds.

PUPIL: All of this sounds very interesting and inspiring. But when I look about me and see the people who are succeeding, and who have so much more in life than I have, it is confusing. They do not seem to know, or care, a thing about God. How about that?

MASTER: If I were you I would try attending to **my own** knitting and start at once to develop my own power; also I would stop envying others their success.

PUPIL: Oh I am not envying anybody anything. I simply do not understand.

MASTER: It would help if you would try to avoid a tailspin of self-pity. As soon as you observe someone who is getting on better than you are you must project yourself into his life critically. Try doing this same thing **constructively.** Explore his tactics, his tastes, his imagination and industry; and then ask yourself if you might not get along better and faster if you adopted some of the means he employs.

PUPIL: How can I know how another does his work to succeed? And I did not realize that I have been feeling sorry for myself. How would it be to try to see myself as others see me?

MASTER: It would help very much if you will turn your imagination on yourself without any excuses or alibis. Your imagination will show you your true self if you have the courage to use it and trust it. And let you intuition help you also.

THIRD SUPPLEMENT
"HOW TO LIVE LIFE AND LOVE IT!"
Children, How to Bring Them Forth If You Wish Them. Home, Husbands, Wives, if You Desire Them.

PUPIL: It seems to me that many of my married friends would be perfectly happy if only children would come to them. It seems strange they can not have any.

MASTER: No, it is not strange. It is all according to Law. "Principle is not governed by precedent." Children are the result of knowing, feeling, living that Law consciously or unconsciously; they are the birth of **new** ideas, something different. Every baby is a **new idea,** a new form in which Life lives. Get into the habit of developing new ideas and you will find these very ideas taking the form of children. It need not matter what the new ideas are about so long as you fully develop them. Then mentally picture as many children as you would like to have. When about to give birth to the new idea in form (a baby) I would suggest the daily help of a really good Mental Science practitioner, also at the time of birth. With proper understanding the birth of the child will be as natural as the spiritual idea which preceded the form.

PUPIL: All of this sounds very wonderful and convincing while I talk with you. At the risk of your thinking my mind a sieve may I ask you to put all three steps, husband, home, children, into concise, separate form.

MASTER: Very well. The idea of concentration is not a leaky one and I shall be happy to present them in the order you name. But first what, exactly what, does the word husband mean to you? What characteristics do you wish the husband to manifest? What should his disposition be in order to be in tune with yours? These are your **very first steps** along the way.

PUPIL: To me husband symbolizes certain characteristics I would like to attract to myself from the masculine side of Life, or quality of Life, a type of man I admire. His main qualities should be, for me, **understanding** and **love.** With these two attributes well-developed in both of us I believe happiness would be certain to follow.

MASTER: With **love** and **understanding** well developed in husband and wife happiness **is certain** to follow. The one certain way to attract this type of husband is to **develop love** and **understanding** in **your self.** It is a very great truth that **like attracts like!** So first think over carefully just the type of man you feel could be happy with you.

PUPIL: Oh, I thought I was to think of the qualities my husband should have to make **me** happy.

MASTER: That method would help to develop self-centeredness, selfishness. But the other way is a **reaching out to GIVE** what you have and has a very great attracting power. When you have determined the type of man whom you feel would be happy with you, then take for yourself an early morning-hour and through reading and meditation **think yourself into** the quality of Life you wish to attract and hold the feeling. Herein lies the real value of holding your thought and feeling into place, just like plugging into the light socket when you want light. If you keep pulling the plug you will not get much light. The secret is: MAKE your contact in thought and feeling and HOLD IT, with a happy, expectant attitude. Of course this ability to hold an idea is arrived at by developing the will.

PUPIL: It seems to me that visualizing will not work unless the mental pictures made are held in place in mind. Is that right?

MASTER: That is exactly right. They **must be** held in place, again just like the electric contact for lights must be held in place if you are to benefit by the light which will then stay on. Your magnet of **thought** and **feeling** draws from out of the whole Universe such qualities as **Love, Understanding, Protection, Provision, husband, children, whatever it is you have visualized.**

PUPIL: It is like a postage-stamp then; it only has value if it sticks. Am I right about this: that what I **really** AM that I ATTRACT? Might this not be the meaning of Jesus' statement in Matthew 13:20 when he said "For whomsoever hath to him shall be given and he shall have more abundance; but whosoever hath not from him shall be taken away even that which he hath?" When one really HAS a husband in **feeling** and mentally pictures him one really does HAVE that husband; and he is SURE to appear in form as a human being: Is this not having more abundance? How slowly I grow. First I wanted my husband to have understanding; now I see that he IS understanding.

MASTER: That is it. Every conceivable thing that the human mind and heart can desire IS already in existence. Like the electricity it has always been there; and as soon as one realizes it and tunes the desire in with that quality of Life which it is the current begins to flow in that direction. Then one has real abundance through continually having the recognition that whatsoever he may want he already has it.

PUPIL: Is the process the same if one wants several children?

MASTER: Yes, fundamentally it is the same. If we wish to manifest our new ideas of Life in the form of children, it is necessary to make the desire known to God, the Great, Ever-Present, Formative, Responsive, Creative, Intelligent Power. It being Responsive and Creative it **manifests in form**, as children.

PUPIL: Just what should one first begin to think and feel?

MASTER: First, let us suppose that your desire for children is in perfect accord with the Divine Plan to bring into earth existence a continual advancement of the human race. So your idea of the new birth is that you may be a **means,** or a **channel,** through which the All-Creating Principle of Intelligent, Beautiful, Perfect Life may reproduce Itself in a new form, one capable of recognizing itself a an individualized action of Pure Spirit. Then by reading good articles or books or by meditating on an affirmation that appeals to you, you tune your thought and **feeling** in with the very highest rate of vibration. Stay with the thought and feeling until you are **certain** that you HAVE made your contact with the Divine Intelligence, just as you are certain that you shall turn on the light when you plug into a light-socket. You know, under the latter circumstance, that the contact IS made because the room is flooded with light. And in the mental instance you know your contact IS made because your whole **feeling** IS flooded with **certainty** and a sense of **security** in God's Love and Power as they manifest in and through you.

PUPIL: It seems to me that one would have to keep constantly in mind the thought of begetting perfect ideas relative to every act.

MASTER: Jesus said: "Watch and pray lest you enter into temptation." You feel towards God (Life) in the same way your child feels toward you. If you obey the Laws of Life because you love your Father (Life) your child will do the same.

PUPIL: Is it necessary that both father and mother should desire the children? Should they take their meditations together? Should they discuss the hope of children?

MASTER: If both father and mother desire children the new idea will be a more perfect idea of God. It is not necessary to take the meditations together. In fact, I personally prefer to have all of my meditations **alone.** And it seems to me the **less** one discusses a desire with **anyone** the more quickly and perfectly the desire manifests. If one talks about a thing usually it is put in the **future** and is rarely discussed as a PRESENT FACT; hence the manifestation is delayed indefinitely because of the habit of looking upon it as a future manifestation, as something that "will be" rather than something that IS.

PUPIL: How is this for a method of bringing children of your own into one's personal life? First, study and think over the fundamental Law of Life as always giving expression to its highest ideals and ideas in human form. Man is God's highest ideal and the children of men are specialized ideas of the One Great Creative Source of all things. Are not our children the results of God's ideas of giving birth to our highest desires?

MASTER: You have the right idea. Try to really feel that God, Life, Love, Wisdom, **is** giving birth to a particular idea through you. **Plant** that idea, that thought-seed, in the garden of your individual sub-conscious mind. By using your individual subconscious quality of mind in this way you are doing your part to let **all** the Creative Energy in the Universe act in and through you without limit. Thus you are a bridge between the two extremes in the scale of Nature, one of which is the innermost Creative Spirit of Life and the other the particular, external form of a child. Your objective quality of thought-power mentally sees your perfect child, then passes the thought and the picture into the creative power of your individual quality of subconscious mind which in turn transfers the thought-seed into ALL of the growing power there is in Life, thus bridging the two extremes of Nature. Your thought-seed will grow into perfect externalization just as a kernel of corn will when planted under the proper conditions.

PUPIL: This idea of a thought-seed clears up the whole idea that my individual subconscious mind is the bridge between myself and the whole vast sea of Life.

MASTER: If you plant a kernel of corn you first make sure the soil and the climate is the proper kind to grow corn.

PUPIL: Does that mean I should look into my own character and physical condition, and so forth, to determine if I really am the type of woman to bear perfect children?

MASTER: You are right. It is vitally important to know these things. Once you have found out that these are clear, and you and your husband are sure in your minds that you wish to create in form your highest ideal of Love, as children, then proceed. Remember that the seed you plant, having all the vitality, all the vital essence, necessary to draw to itself from out of All Life every element necessary to cause it to grow into a perfect outward reproduction, a perfect child. Every parent, or parent-to-be, should be an **enlightened** parent, of course, and should do all within the power to bring forth, cherish, nurture and rear, the finest children possible. It will help those who are, or who desire to be, parents if they will **inform** themselves fully along the most scientific lines on this question. This they may do in numerous ways, through the reading of good books on the subject, ones that are written by specialists, also by taking courses on the subject that are offered almost continually through university-extension plans, also in many places by city and state departments; and lastly to seek the advice and care of the best physicians from conception forward.

FOURTH SUPPLEMENT
"HOW TO LIVE LIFE AND LOVE IT!"
Life, Love, Beauty

MASTER: In his wonderful books Judge Troward stresses often that the Spirit of Life also is one of Love and Beauty, and that where the One is the others will be found, too, as a matter of necessity. Where Life is Love is. One is the correlative of the other. Where Life and Love are Beauty must be.

PUPIL: May we have another illustration to clarify this?

MASTER: Certainly. All persons have an appreciation of art. The ancient Greeks were supreme in the arts for many centuries. To this day many of their works have never been equaled. I have never seen that fact more compellingly illustrated than it was one day last summer at our home on The Esplanade, Redondo Beach, California. A gentleman friend of Mr. Smith's (Worth Smith, my husband) who, like Mr. Smith, has been a student of the Great Pyramid for many years, called on us. He brought a wonderful book and showed us many lovely pictures of exquisite Greek vases. Alongside each photograph was a sketch of the same vase with the basic design highlighted in geometry, many lines drawn to salient features of the sketch. Of all the grace and beauty and absolute perfection of symmetry I have ever seen, or hope to, those pictures and sketches had it, without a solitary flaw in any of them. Each was **purest**

harmony, so much so that one marveled and it seemed that **music** itself flowed from them. Each vase was an **expression of God** and His laws of Life, Love, Beauty and Harmony, executed to perfection by artists in whom His Love, Beauty, Harmony LIVED. Because of their **adoration** of Beauty, and its Source in the Father, they were able to **conceive** Beauty in the mind when planning the designs of the vases. No doubt they sketched the designs as shown in the book, by employment of the geometry in which they excelled. With the **model** before them they then **fashioned** the works of superb Harmony to glorify the earth. Wherever perfect Harmony is there you will find perfect Love for they are twin blessings!

PUPIL: But all of us can not make such masterpieces, you know, for all of us do not have such artistic talents. Do we?

MASTER: All of us have **some** talent within us. Unfortunately, many seem to never realize it and never **do** anything about it. Even so any person of intelligence **can** put into **whatever task** that one may have to do the Spirit of Life, Love, Beauty and Harmony, IF only one will, and can make of the **fruits** of the task many things of Beauty. Some housewives, for example, make of housekeeping and rearing children a thing of drudgery as a result of their lack of illumination about the **true divinity** of housekeeping. Others put Love, Beauty, Harmony, Order and Joy into the same task and make a glory of it. It is a matter of the **spiritual consciousness** one **has,** or **acquires through study** if it is not there innately.

PUPIL: Will you please cite an example from the Bible which features this matter of **consciousness** of our divinity as being the root of all blessings?

MASTER: Gladly indeed. Study carefully St. Matthew, chapter 13, verse 12. Jesus uttered those golden words to teach man-kind that **like does attract like,** INvariably and INfallibly. That passage states the **law of attraction** at its best, including an unshakable **faith,** visualizing by means of which one HAS **spiritually,** or in the mind, even that which is sought, and which serves as a **magnet of infinite power** to draw to one the **glad fulfillment in form,** or physical reality, provided only one also WORKS confidently and happily to carry out the ideas the Father gives one, through intuition, as steps in the path to the shining goal.

Now let us directly quote the passage, then strip it bare of all the "mystery" so many claim it contains for them. Unfortunately, to many that verse remains a riddle for life unless they are sufficiently interested to seek until they find the key to its solution. The passage reads:

> "For whosoever HATH, **to him** shall be **given,** and he shall have **more abundance:** but whosoever hath NOT from him shall be **taken away** even that he hath."

The big question is: "For whosoever hath" **what?** Does it mean the one who has wealth of money, or property, or other earthly possessions? **No,** although the one who has the thing that is meant is certain to **acquire** financial independence and retain it. It means simply that "whosoever hath" the CONSCIOUSNESS of the **Father within,** who has that **exalted awareness** as an **abiding conviction,** who has **implicit faith** in it, and who **actively carries on in the work** that one does, **whatever** it may be, the **ideas** of Life, Love, Beauty and Harmony the Father gives that one in an UNending stream, to **that one** will be GIVEN ALL he may ever require, and **to spare.** But the person who "hath **not"** the high consciousness is subject to all the sorrows, lacks and other inharmonies circumstances and conditions can bring to bear upon him, even to the point of losing all he has gained through habitual employment of **secondary** causation. . . for since he has **not** the awareness he is, or shall be, "under the rule of an iron destiny," to quote Troward, and dwells in anxiety and fear, knowing **not** that "the eternal God is our refuge and a very present help in trouble."

PUPIL: Can that Love, Beauty and Harmony be caused to flow from one person, a practitioner let us say, into and through another so that the second party will be aware of the spiritual uplift, and receive corresponding benefits?

MASTER: Yes, indeed, that is done easily. That is the mission of the practitioner, for he or she does these things for others many hours a day. I well recall an incident that occurred not long ago in the beautiful home of a dearly beloved friend and student in Denver. I was sitting with her privately in her lovely living-room, holding her left hand in my right, thus **completing a circuit** exactly as an electric circuit is made, positive pole in contact with the negative pole. With my mind I made contact with the Love, Beauty and Harmony the Spirit is. From the Universal Spirit of Life those **qualities** flowed into me, and through me into my dear friend, and through her back into the Universal. For minutes we kept the contact and both of us were aware of the surge of **tremendous power** flowing through us. I have this friend's kind permission to mention her name. She is Grace N. Northcutt. It is she whose gracious generosity accounts for the new edition of this book you are now reading.

PUPIL: Then it is true that as one makes of it a **habit** to **consciously recognize** God in one's daily, hourly, even **minute-by-minute living** in that degree one will **get good results?**

MASTER: Yes. The **correspondence is exact!** As we apply the laws of electricity we are certain to get results that correspond to those laws **only.** It is folly to apply one set of creative laws to a problem and expect to get results that correspond to a **different** code. So it is that if we set in motion through concentrated and consecrated **thinking** the laws of Harmony then **only Harmony** will manifest in and through us, and in our affairs!

Again I give you the golden key which will unlock **any** door of bondage and which will never disappoint you if you persist in the use of it in wisdom. It is, I repeat, that twelfth verse of the thirteen chapter of Matthew.

PUPIL: How is it obtained? What price does one have to pay for the key?

MASTER: The price is given in the fifteenth chapter of John and is, as Jesus said: "ABIDE IN ME!" That will put you in an entirely new relationship to your Father and to your environment, will open up many new possibilities hitherto undreamed of, all by an orderly sequence of creative laws that result from your new mental attitude. **Thought** is the energy by which the law of attraction is brought into operation. It is by **thought** that we keep the sap of life flowing from the trunk into the branches. The statement Jesus made in Matthew 13:12 is so important that He made it repeatedly, worded a bit differently, yet containing the self-same law He expressed therein.

PUPIL: May we have a schedule, and some affirmations, for daily use? If we have one before us, in print, it should help a lot, it seems to me, in our follow-through.

MASTER: First I shall give you two affirmations I have found very effective and powerful when **consistently** used with **profound feeling.**

1. "Father, I thank Thee for the **conscious** knowledge that **all my good comes from Thee only,** and that I no longer look to man as the source of my supply!"

2. **"God** IS **my ever-present supply** and large sums of money come to me quickly, under grace and in perfect ways, so to **bountifully supply my every need,** and to   spare!"

Moreover a careful study of these three references will be a great aid, i.e., Mark 5:36 and 9:23, John 20:29.

Lastly, I am happy to give you an excellent routine for daily use that Troward himself gave to me. I have used it faithfully for thirty-five years now and it is a powerful help indeed. It is this:

Monday . . . **Watch your words!**

Tuesday . . . **Watch your feeling!**

Wednesday . . . **Watch your acts!**

Thursday. . . **Watch your receiving!**

Friday . . . **Watch your giving!**

Saturday . . . **Look for** the Spirit of Life and Love in **everybody** and in **everything!**

Sunday . . . **Let the Lord's Prayer** abide with you **continually!**

Hypnotic Marketing Library Collection from Joe Vitale

"These are the secrets you need if you want to create marketing messages (ads, articles, sales letters, emails etc.) that make your prospects stand up and take action...

"Who Else Wants To Learn A Simple, Step-By-Step 'System' For Crafting <u>Hypnotic Marketing Messages</u> That Practically Force YOUR Prospects To Whip Out Their Plastic - Every Time?

"If You Seriously Want To Take Your Business To The NEXT Level... Read Every Word On This Page and Find Out How YOU Can Apply These 'Time-Tested' and *Proven Marketing Secrets* Into YOUR Business..."

Are you serious about your Internet marketing success? Do you want to achieve results in your business that you know you're capable of, but have eluded you until now?

Joe Vitale is **the real deal**. His **Hypnotic Marketing** techniques have created amazing results for Joe and his clients, and now you can take advantage of his incredible knowledge with the **Hypnotic Marketing Library Super Package CD-ROM**. And, you can shave $224 off the price of Joe's complete hypnotic marketing collection when you **take advantage of this special collection price** now.

Over the years, Joe has built quite a reputation for his marketing prowess. If you wanted to hire Joe to just give you some advice, you would pay $500 an hour. Want Joe Vitale to write you a sales letter? It would cost you $12,500 and up. How about a website critique? This would cost you $650 to start.

If this sounds a little steep, it's not. Joe charges this much because he's worth it. Joe has tons of happy clients who know he's **worth every single penny** they shell out because Joe's marketing techniques and advice always create a **huge return on their investment**. Just look at what some of the top marketers on the Internet are saying about Joe:

> "If you can't pull a $50,000 idea out of this e-book you'd better put a mirror to your face and see if it fogs ups. Joe pounds and blitzes you with one incredible idea, story and example after another. My brain was on overload! I give it an A+."
>
> —Yanik Silver, SurefireMarketing.com

> "Joe Vitale hypnotized me today! He did it with 'Hypnotic Marketing,' which I found impossible to stop reading. I learned something new on every page, and I've been learning about marketing since 1958. Now, I can only shudder for those poor souls who haven't yet learned what Joe has to teach. Not only does he enlighten, but he does it in such a warm and engaging way, that you cannot help but   complete his book with a smile in your heart and dollar signs on your mind. Thank you, Joe, for a mighty contribution to the world of marketing."
>
> —Jay Conrad Levinson, author
> Guerrilla Marketing series

> "Joe, you've written a masterpiece. Condensing the formula for getting rich in only 79 days into three simple steps anyone can follow is brilliant! As with everything you write, 'Hypnotic Marketing' is crammed full of true-to-life, straight forward ways to start a welcome flow of cash into anyone's bank account. We all thank you for making this gem available. But, come on, Joe... that price. You've got to be kidding! Why would you give

away so much for so little? It's like selling Fort Knox at a discount!"

—Dr. Paul Hartunian
How to Get a Million
Dollars in Publicity FREE!

"Do what 'Hypnotic Marketing' says and you will get rich! It's simply brilliant! I learn something that increases my bottom line profits every time I read Joe Vitale. 'Hypnotic Marketing' is an ENCYCLOPEDIA of specific laser beam strategies of how to market your business NOW. Trust me. I know. The last time I used just ONE of Joe Vitale's ideas in a marketing plan I earned $12,865 in one DAY! (That's just one idea!)"

—Kevin Hogan, Author,
The Psychology of Persuasion

"I finished reading 'Hypnotic Marketing' last night and I just have one question: Pardon my French, Joe, but Jesus Christ, do you have ANY secrets left? I've never seen anybody reveal as many of their secrets in one fell swoop as you did in this book. The only way you could put money in your readers' pockets any faster is if you wrote them a check yourself! My favorite chapter is number 29 on Gold Mine.net. The before and after illustration is dramatic to say the least. Your revised copy is awesome, but when you compare it against the original it is even more so. Also, I really liked your muscle test section. It's a new and fascinating idea. Maybe you'll start a new trend with this one!"

—Blair Warren, Author
The Forbidden Keys to Persuasion

"Awesome! Joe's new book lays out a complete, navigable road map for the marketing novice and veteran alike. You'll find loads of valuable information and specific techniques here. Plus, there are several gems in this book -- like the 5 ways to get people to open an email, and the 5 ways to start a killer email sales letter -- that is each worth at least 10 times the price of the book itself.

Unless you are a billionaire whose only problem is that you have too much money, you need this book!"

—David Garfinkel, Author
Advertising Headlines That Make You Rich

But, thanks to Nitro Marketing, you don't have to shell out the big bucks to get the inside scoop on Joe's Hypnotic Marketing techniques.

Working with Joe, we've created the ultimate Hypnotic Marketing resource -- the **Hypnotic Marketing Library Super Package.**

We've crammed **ten of Joe's best Hypnotic ebooks onto a single CD-ROM**, giving you access to some of the best marketing and copywriting resources that have been produced in the last century. If you had to purchase all 10 of these great products separately, you would have to pay $620.

But because we were able to convince Joe to work with us on this Package, we were able to "twist his arm" and get him to allow us to offer all 10 of these great ebooks on a single CD-ROM for the **incredible price of only $397** (plus s/h). That's a **whopping 40% savings.**

Let's take a small peek into exactly what you will be learning when you take advantage of this very special offer today...

The Hypnotic Marketing Library Super Package

Here's what you'll receive when you order Joe Vitale's Hypnotic Marketing Library Super Package on CD-ROM:

☑ **Hypnotic Writing and Advanced Hypnotic Writing**

Joe shares with you all of the powerful secrets to crafting hypnotic sales materials and also teaches you advanced persuasion techniques that have earned him and his students millions of dollars **(Value: $37 + $67)**

Here's a small sample of what you will learn...

- Learn the top hypnotic secrets that master hypnotists have been **jealously guarding** – which **empower** you to get all the orders you desire from your customers

- How to easily lead your prospect into a hypnotic state, and **program** him to be receptive to your offer – without his realizing you're doing it

- How to skillfully enter the **hypnotic threshold** of your prospects' minds so that they will accept, act upon, and *obey your commands*

- The top 3 things you must do to satisfy a **primal** need that lies deep within your prospects – and make them want to buy whatever you're selling

- How to **secretly** penetrate your prospect's **subconscious mind** and fill it with your powerful hypnotic suggestions

- How to instill in your prospects a **visceral** need they can feel at the **gut level** – and create a desire for a resolution that only your product or service can satisfy

- How to dazzle people with hypnotic sales letters that make them follow your commands

- How to use **outrageous** creativity as a hypnotic mechanism to pull in more sales

- Learn the ultimate secret to controlling the **public mind** – is a diabolical principle of **hidden selling** that creates cash automatically outside of human perception

- Hidden commands you can use to make people do your bidding

- **8 hypnotic devices** you can use immediately to get a guaranteed "yes" to your offer

- The 7 deadly things marketers do that make their prospects "snap out" of the hypnotic state and make the sales process grind to a screeching halt

- How to **melt** the resistance of even the most stubborn prospect. (This slick hypnotic technique moves mountains).

- Learn the greatest hypnotic secret ever revealed – this is an advertising "formula" that is absolutely indispensable as you embark on your hypnotic marketing expedition

- How to install a *post-hypnotic suggestion* in your readers' brains so that if they can't buy right now, they will be hypnotically compelled to *buy later*

- How to write intriguing headlines that cast a **spell** on your reader

- What to write in your website that makes people want to visit it, talk about it, and then, in the end, **buy whatever you are selling**

- Learn how to **saturate** your writing with intense, emotion-provoking language that sells every time

- Learn the exact words you can use in a sales letter that will make your customers whip out their wallets and buy from you

- How to write **tantalizing** copy that makes your reader's mouth water with anticipation

- Learn the psychological tricks that make your sales letters impossible to ignore

- Discover little-known hypnotic language patterns that literally **dissolve** your prospect's objections

- Get the **Top-Secret** Checklist – Joe Vitale uses this to pre-test the hypnotic quotient of his letters – pure gold!

- How to write a hypnotic headline – in under 15 seconds

- How to craft embedded commands in your writing that make people feel compelled to act now

- How to create **mesmerizing** stories and scenarios that grab the attention of your reader, and hold him captive all the way to the order page

- Discover the little-known **loophole** in the public's mind that allows you to easily engage your prospects hypnotically

- How to drop hypnotic cues in your prospects' subconscious that create an **instinctive** desire for your product or service

- What hypnotic strategies work online, but not offline – and vice versa

- Create your own hypnotic news releases using these proven models

- How to exploit the one proven hypnotic ad format that always works

- How to use **hypnotic suggestion** to compel editors to call within minutes of receiving your press release

- Plus much, much more...

☑ Hypnotic Marketing

Marketing techniques on how to make your publicity, emails and websites hypnotic. **(Value: $67)**

The table of contents alone will reflect just how much is in this work...

STEP ONE: HYPNOTIC PUBLICITY

Chapter 2: How to Hypnotize the Masses with "PO" Ideas

Chapter 3: Flying Midgets and the PR Folk Hero

Chapter 4: **Eight Proven Rules** for Getting Publicity

Chapter 5: Pitching a Heavyweight Boxing Champion and His Sausage

Chapter 6: Show Your Bra!

Chapter 7: 21 Ways to Identify Story Ideas About You or Your Business

Chapter 8: Running Water

Chapter 9: Selling Bloody Games

Chapter 10: One of the Easiest Ways in the World to Get Publicity

Chapter 11: How to Install a "Success Wish" in Your Mind

Chapter 12: The Top Three Ways **Guaranteed to ALWAYS Hypnotize** the Media

Chapter 13: 10 Tips on Becoming Newsworthy from a Media Tigress

Chapter 14: The Seven Laws of Baseball's Greatest Publicist

Chapter 15: The Psychology of Hypnotic Publicity

Chapter 16: Edgy Top Secret Ways to Absolutely Nail Media Attention

Chapter 17: How to Get Rich With **P.T. Barnum's Secret**

Chapter 18: The Amazing Breakthrough Formula Called "E-DR Publicity"

Chapter 34: How to Create E-mails that **Secretly Seduce Your Readers**

Chapter 35: The Five Best Ways to Create Hypnotic Email Openers

Chapter 36: "How Can the Right Question Bring in 317% More Orders?"

Chapter 37: E-mail Sales Letter Samples that are Making Me Rich

Chapter 38: A **Little Known Secret for Doubling Responses** to Your E-Offers

Chapter 39: How to Make Even More Money With This Unusual E-mail Secret

Chapter 40: What are Five Ways to Get People to Open Your E-mail?

Chapter 41: A Truly "Killer" Hypnotic Sales Letter Used Online AND Off

Chapter 42: The World's Most Unusual Way to Strengthen Your Hypnotic Writing

BONUSES:

Bonus #1: How to Create a **Hypnotic** Viral Marketing Campaign

Bonus #2: The 10 Most Dangerous Marketing Books of All Time

Bonus #3: How to Create Your Own Hypnotic Business Cards

Bonus #4: **Dangerous Selling** -- A New Way to Increase Your Profits

Bonus #5: What Bernice Taught Me About Advertising

Bonus #6: How to Create Sales After Creating Relationships

Bonus #7: The **Three Real Secrets** to Success Today

Epilogue: The Hidden Secret to Getting Rich -- *In Only 79 Days*

☑ **Hypnotic Writer's Swipe File**

Joe Vitale's personal swipe file of over 1550 copywriting gems that have been proven in the trenches. **(Value: $197)**

Previously, only a trusted few had access to and were able to benefit from the Hypnotic Writer's Swipe File -- and now you can too. Here are just a few of the ways you'll benefit:

- 2 irresistible mind-grabbing words that are **the most powerful copywriting words** of all time and should be used repeatedly in your copy to get immediate results.

- 5 hypnotic agreement questions that will **put prospects in a *"yes" trance*** where they will be conditioned to agree with your next statements.

- 31 hypnotic headline words that will get your sales copy read and can drastically increase your sales.

- 178 psychological copy connectors that you can weave into sentences and paragraphs to **compel** readers to take the actions you want.

- 5 hidden commands that are so good, people won't even realize you are **secretly commanding them.**

- 7 "confusers to take control" statements that will confuse readers and allow your hypnotic words to **get past their mental censors.**

- 5 forbidden hypnotic words that will **slip right into your readers' minds** just because they end in "ly."

- 33 subliminal closings/P.S.'s that will *persuade undecided readers* to order your product immediately.

- 163 emotional provoking words that can **trigger your prospects**' emotions and persuade them to buy your product.

- 860 fill-in-the-blank sentence starters that will **reel in your readers** and get them in the proper state of mind to buy your product.

- Insert any of these 11 powerful **embedded commands** into your sentences to compel people to **obey** you. These are so sneaky -- your prospects will never see them coming!

- Dominate your prospect with 13 hypnotic hype action phrases that surround your offer with an **invisible field of magnetism** that very few people can resist.

- Slip these 5 **forbidden** hypnotic words before your command -- and people will feel compelled to do **exactly** what you say.

- Discover 32 camouflaged headline templates that **disguise** your ad as **riveting** editorial content -- thereby skyrocketing the readership of your ad.

- Discover 63 hypnotic opening statements that **take command** of your prospects' mind, put them under your spell -- and keep them tantalized by every word of your sales letter.

- 7 hypnotic devices that make your prospects virtually "dizzy" with information that they have no recourse but to agree with **whatever you propose**.

- 1 simple prefixes that **disguise** your command as a gentle statement -- thereby making it immensely likely that your prospect will follow your hidden command

- 7 "stop commands" that immediately grab your prospect's attention and make him receptive to any hypnotic suggestion you say next.

- 3 hypnotic story-telling methods that mesmerize people -- and lead them to do exactly what you want.

- Countless **specialized communication patterns** that cast a spell on your prospects, and make them want to do whatever you say.

- 41 bullet modifications that elevate **excitement** and **curiosity** -- and make your bullets even more powerful.

- Choose from 22 visual, auditory and kinesthetic phrases that give you the exact language patterns that appeal to any type of prospect.

- 55 "logic generators" give validity to anything you write -- use these words to get people to respect you as an authority or a leader – a person to be listened to, admired and followed.

☑ **Hypnotic Selling Tools**

Receive 1739 proven to be effective hypnotic words, phrases and sentences you can use today to instantly make your material hypnotic. **(Value: $47)**

Say the following to yourself, out loud: By reading this powerful ebook you will quickly learn:

... *800 hypnotic sentence starters* that will bypass your prospect's conscious mind and **persuade their subconscious mind to order your product.**

... Uncover *440 mesmerizing copy connectors* that will release the floodgates of your prospect's mind and **lead them straight to your order page.**

... Possess *60 subconscious openers* that will **crack open your prospect's subconscious mind** and make them receptive to your suggestions.

... Own *25 seductive story starters* that will **pull your prospects directly into your sales letter.**

... Discover **131 embedded commands and benefits** that will be persuasive and totally invisible to your prospects!

... Know **21 psychic influences that will telepathically penetrate your prospect's mind** over the Internet!

... Hold **19 sensory persuaders** that will **give convincing proof to anything** you write!

... Learn **12 unforeseen closes** that will **mysteriously close each sale** without your prospects realizing it!

... Extract **16 penetrating P.S.'s** that will help **loosen your prospect's mental buying defenses** and give them confidence in purchasing!

... Unearth **160 mind opening questions** that will **automatically unlock your prospect's brain** and trigger persuasive, mental movies!

... Find out **20 unorthodox suggestions** that **will influence your prospect's mind to absorb and believe your information!**

... Use **25 forbidden benefits** that will **condition your prospects to persuade themselves to buy!**

... Master **10 emotional triggers** that will **arouse your prospect's inner buying feelings!**

... And **be gloriously RICH!**

☑ **How to Write Hypnotic Articles**

Shows you how to get free publicity by writing hypnotic articles that people want to publish. **(Value: $37)**

Would you settle for being able to write a hypnotic article in less than 7 minutes? Yes? Well, good, because here's just 17 things you'll learn...

1. The **17 benefits of writing and submitting free reprint articles** to e-zines and websites

2. **The secret formula** for writing articles at warp speed

3. How to **quickly and easily roll out** one or two articles every week

4. *30 possible reasons* your article won't get published

5. How to **persuade someone else to write** most of your articles for you -- for free

6. How to **put your article writing on auto pilot**

7. 10 ways to **increase the perceived value of your article**

8. How to **avoid writer's block** all together

9. How to write articles with just a few clicks of your mouse

10. How to write articles **regardless of your writing ability**

11. How to **write totally original articles**

12. *11 fast and effortless ways* to write articles

13. How to **cut your article writing time** into virtually just a few minutes

14. How to have your articles **practically write themselves**

15. How to write an article by sending *just one simple e-mail message*

16. How to **get free advertising** writing your own articles

17. **6 ways** to persuade other people to **write articles for you for free** or for no upfront costs

☑ **How to Write Hypnotic Joint Venture Proposals**

Shows you how to use hypnotic principles to pull in lucrative joint ventures that produce a huge number of sales, commissions and signups. **(Value: $37)**

Here's just some of the information that's inside...

- The 7 most popular types of joint venture deals. You probably haven't even thought of some of these. *(See Chapter 1)*

- Find out who your first resource should be, plus 18 others people who will want to sell your products for you. *(See Chapter 2)*

- Know exactly what your joint venture prospect needs and wants most from you -- and get a list of 25 specific needs and wants your joint venture prospects have. *(See Chapter 2)*

- Where to find qualified and targeted joint venture partners -- and how to know exactly what they want from you. *(See Chapter 2)*

- How to evaluate a joint venture candidate to make sure they can help you. *(See Chapter 3)*

- How to **pre-sell your hypnotic proposal** before you even send it. *(See Chapter 3)*

- How to **subconsciously** persuade people to accept your proposal -- and the 6 words that will make your offer irresistible. *(See Chapter 4)*

- Know what to say when you are negotiating a joint venture proposal -- even when they want more than you're willing to offer. *(See Chapter 5)*

- How to put the odds in your favor even if they don't accept your offer. *(See Chapter 5)*

- How to get **free products and services** from your joint venture deals. *(See Chapter 6)*

- Get **36 templates** that will influence your prospects to read the rest of your proposal and accept your joint venture offer. These can be altered for any offer. *(See Chapter 6)*

☑ **How to Write Hypnotic Endorsements**

Shows you how to easily write hypnotic endorsements to pull in huge sales, commissions and signups. **(Value: $37)**

Here's just some of the information that's inside...

- How to **pick the most profitable products, services and affiliate programs to endorse**

- **A simple 7 step formula** for writing your very first personal endorsement

- **290 fill in the blank personal endorsement templates** that will allow you to write an endorsement in just minutes

- **20 specific tips** for writing a hypnotic personal endorsement

- How to **transform your personal endorsements into multiple marketing tools**

- 12 ways to **make your endorsements credible** even if you're not an expert

- How to **virtually eliminate your competition** even if you're reselling the same product

☑ **Hypnotic Selling Stories**

Shows you how to easily write hypnotic stories that people relate with, builds their trust in you and increases sales and signups. **(Value: $47)**

Here's a few things you'll learn when you read HSS...

- How to write Hypnotic Selling Stories with little or no writing

- A Step-By-Step Example of How to Create a Hypnotic Selling Story

- What Everyone Will Always Read

- Joe's Secrets for Writing Hypnotic Selling Stories?

- 80 Hypnotic Selling Story Ideas that Sell!

- 58 Formulas for Creating a Hypnotic Selling Story

- How to Turn Your Selling Stories Into Multiple Marketing Tools and much, much more...

☑ **Hypnotic Traffic Tools**

Shows you how to use hypnotic tools to generate massive traffic to your websites. **(Value: $47)**

Here's a sneak-peek at a few things you'll find out about...

- The **Amazing Benefits** of Creating Hypnotic Traffic Tools

- The Most Popular Types of *Hypnotic Traffic Tools*

- **15 Places** to Find YOUR Next Hypnotic Traffic Idea

- 12 Reasons People Won't Use Your Hypnotic Traffic Tools

- **99 Ways to Persuade People** to Use Your Hypnotic Traffic Tools

- How to Easily Create Hypnotic Traffic Tools *Without Writing Them Yourself!*

- **16 Important Elements** to Include In Your "Content Requests"

- 10 Places to Send Your "Content Requests"

- *11 Ways to Persuade People to Give Up Their Ideas*

TOTAL VALUE = $620.00

GO TO

www.HypnoticMarketingStrategy.com

AND ORDER TODAY!

In all, this very special offer brings you a total of **$851.00 worth of products and discounts** -- worth thousands more in true value to you and your business -- for only $397 (plus s/h). And, since we offer a **100%**

unconditional 60-day money-back guarantee, there is no way you can lose with the **Hypnotic Marketing Library Super Package**.

If you want to **take your business to the next level**, you need to increase the effectiveness of every dollar that you spend. With the Hypnotic Marketing Library, you will have all the tools needed to experience:

- Staggering increases in sales and sign-ups
- Out of this world conversion rates
- Sites swamped with free, targeted traffic
- Prospects compelled to reach for their wallet
- Sales letters written quickly and effortlessly

So **get a copy of Joe Vitale's Hypnotic Marketing Library Super Package** today and save 40% on the most important collection of marketing materials we've ever put together. This one CD-ROM could help you turn your business into a cash machine that *consistently pulls in business*, day after day, month after month. **Order Your Copy Right Now!**

P.S. This offer has a **100% unconditional money-back guarantee**. If you don't see the value in Joe Vitale's *Hypnotic Marketing Library Super Package* on CD-ROM, for any reason whatsoever, you can return it in the first 60 days for a **prompt and courteous refund. So get your package today!**

Here's what the legendary Joe Sugarman says:

"All the tools and phrases are here for even the inexperienced to construct a powerful message. If you're serious about direct marketing, this is a great book to read and study."

About the Authors

Photograph by Julie Eskoff

Dr. Joe Vitale, President of Hypnotic Marketing, Inc., located outside of Austin, Texas, is the author of way too many books to list here. Here are just a few of them:

He wrote the #1 bestseller, *The Attractor Factor: 5 Easy Steps for Creating Wealth (or anything else) from the Inside Out*, the #3 bestseller *The Greatest Money-Making Secret in History*, and the #1 best-selling E-book *Hypnotic Writing*.

His latest book, written with Jo Han Mok, is *The E-Code: 33 Internet Superstars Reveal 43 Ways to Make Money Online Almost Instantly – with just e-mail.*

His next book will be *Life's Missing Instruction Manual: The Guidebook You Should Have Been Given at Birth.*

Besides all of his books, Dr. Vitale also recorded the #1 best-selling Nightingale-Conant audio program, *The Power of Outrageous Marketing.*

In addition, he has a complete home-study course in marketing at www.HypnoticMarketingStrategy.com.

Sign up for his complimentary newsletter *News You Can Use!* at his main website at www.mrfire.com and visit his new corporate site at www.HypnoticMarketingInc.com

Genevieve Behrend was the only personal pupil of Judge Troward, and she had written the new and practical presentation of the Troward Mental Science, giving the very methods for realizing one's ideals and desires which he himself taught her.

The sages of the ages have united in declaring this great truth: That there is in every human being a source of wisdom and power which we contact through THOUGHT. A Greater Self who can guide and direct us aright. Who can help solve our most vexing problems.

Those who learn to let this Great Self find expression through their lives, find peace, joy, health, success in the truest sense.

Order More Copies of *How to Attain Your Desires* and help change the life of someone else!

Choose from 3 simple ways of ordering today:

1. Visit your favorite bookseller or
3. Visit www.morganjamespublishing.com or
2. Fill out this order form and return to:
Morgan James Publishing, LLC
Post Office Box 6504
Newport News, Virginia 23606

Name: _____

Address: _____

City: _____ State: _____

Zip: _____ Country: _____

Phone: _____ Quantity: _____

Email: _____

Make Check or US Money Order payable to: Morgan James Publishing, LLC

ISBN 0975857088 - *Vol. I - How to Attain Your Desires By Letting Your Subconscious Mind Work For You*

ISBN 1933596325 - *Vol. II - How To Attain Your Desires: How to Live Life and Love It!*

Also Check Out These NEW Titles:

ISBN 097684916X - *At Your Command* by Neville with Dr. Joe Vitale

ISBN 0976849119 - *The Seven Lost Secrets of Success*

($19.95US +$2.92US shipping/handling each)

A New Way To Achieve Your Goals

"To manifest success in any endeavor, there is always a spiritual component — a part of our success that isn't always obvious to the casual observer. Joe Vitale clearly demonstrates how he has effectively recognized and used this spiritual component with amazing success and how you can easily adapt it to fit your life as well — all in five easy steps. I can personally attest to this process and its effectiveness."

~**Joe Sugarman**, Chairman, BluBlocker Corporation

*"'**The Attractor Factor**' is the missing 'owner's manual' for your mind. By using Dr. Vitale's five simple steps, you can regain control of your beliefs and learn to focus your intentions to create the life you really want."*

~**Pat O'Bryan**, Director, The Milagro Research Institute

"A radical and wonderful new way to achieve any goal. I can't wait to put it into practice."

~**Shel Horowitz**, author, *Principled Profit: Marketing That Puts People First*

The Attractor Factor is available at AttractorFactor.com.